BUILD TO OUTPERFORM
Unchain And Unleash A High Performing Team

AJAY BAKSHI

STARDOM BOOKS

STARDOM BOOKS

WORLDWIDE

www.StardomBooks.com

STARDOM BOOKS

A Division of Stardom Publishing

and infoYOGIS Technologies.

105-501 Silverside Road

Wilmington, DE 19809

Copyright © 2022 by Ajay Bakshi

All rights reserved, including right to reproduce this book or portions thereof in any form whatsoever.

FIRST EDITION JANUARY 2022

Stardom Books

Build To Outperform
Unchain And Unleash A High Performing Team

AJAY BAKSHI

p. 246
cm. 15.24 cm x 22.86 cm

Category:

BUS030000 : BUSINESS & ECONOMICS / Human Resources & Personnel Management

BUS071000   BUSINESS & ECONOMICS / Leadership

ISBN: 978-1-957456-03-4

DEDICATION

I would like to dedicate this book to my entire family, starting from my father, Dr J S Bakshi and my mother Dr. and Mrs. Indu Bakshi. My brother Uday Bakshi and my sister-in-law, Puja Bakshi. My mentor and role model Mr. Sandeep Bakhshi and my sister Mrs. Mona Bakhshi. My loving nieces, Laxmi and Durga. Your support, belief and guidance has made this journey much more memorable.
I would also like to remember, Late Mr. S S Puri, Ex DGP ACB, for being my guiding force, an exceptional leader and a source of inspiration.
Finally, I would also like to thank my readers. Hoping that this book inspires you to begin a wonderful journey of your own.

CONTENTS

Acknowledgments i

Foreword ii

INTRODUCTION 1

PART A: SETTING UP HIGH PERFORMING TEAMS

1. WHY SHOULD WE CREATE HIGH PERFORMING TEAMS? — 7
2. CHALLENGES IN CREATING HIGH PERFORMING TEAMS — 17
3. OVERCOMING CHALLENGES IN CREATING HIGH PERFORMING TEAMS — 37
4. DEFINING HIGH PERFORMANCE IN TEAMS AND SETTING PERFORMANCE STANDARDS AND GOALS — 55

PART B: DEVELOPING HIGH PERFORMANCE TEAMS

5. ATTRACTING TALENT AND RECRUITING A HIGH-PERFORMING TEAM — 71
6. DEVELOPING TALENT TO CREATE A HIGH PERFORMING TEAM — 89
7. RETAINING & SUSTAINING HIGH PERFORMANCE — 103

8	ENGAGING AND MOTIVATING HIGH PERFORMING TEAMS	121
9	THE ROLE OF PERFORMANCE MANAGEMENT IN CREATING AND SUSTAINING HIGH-PERFORMING TEAMS	129
10	DEVELOPING YOUR LEADERSHIP CAPABILITY IN LEADING AND INSPIRING OTHERS	143
11	COACHING	161
12	BUILDING A LEADERSHIP PIPELINE AND SUCCESSORS	173

PART C: MAINTAINING HIGH PERFORMANCE TEAMS

13	CREATING HIGH PERFORMING VIRTUAL TEAMS	191
14	MANAGING DIVERSITY AND INCLUSION	203
15	CREATING A CULTURE OF HIGH PERFORMANCE	215
	CONCLUSION	225
	REFERENCES	231
	ABOUT THE AUTHOR	233

ACKNOWLEDGMENTS

I'm thankful for Mr. Dhruba Mukherjee, Dy CEO, Anand Bazar Patrika. Mr. Judhajit Das, CHRO, ICICI Prudential Life Insurance Company Ltd. And Mrs. Anjali Vaishal, Country Manager of a global consulting firm, for all their encouragement. I would like to thank them for sharing their perspectives in a personal capacity which has indeed gone a long way in reinforcing the guiding principles that create a high performing organization.

And finally, to everyone who has been a part of this book and my journey, you are highly appreciated. Your valuable contribution will always be remembered.

FOREWORD

Teamwork is the backbone of civilizations, organizations, and the family unit. In recent years, teamwork has taken center stage in organizations. Leaders are making efforts to understand, define and shape teams and teamwork that help their businesses. There have been numerous concepts, principles and ideas on this vast topic and literally, everyday a new perspective is being shared with the world.

In this regard, it gives me immense pleasure to recommend **Build to Outperform** by Ajay Bakshi, Managing Director/Founder of Metaunlimited and President of Intelligent Leadership Coaching International (ILCI)-India. Ajay is a friend, business partner, and truly an outstanding HR thought leader and executive coach. In this book, Ajay has done an outstanding job covering the guiding principles on how to build and sustain high performing teams.

I believe this book's timing could not be better as the pandemic has heightened our global need to better understand and find meaning in teamwork, whether it is for our business or the small family, which is the crucible of our society. We are facing an increasingly VUCA world, which is Volatile, Uncertain, Complex and Ambiguous. Technology is rapidly redefining how we engage with each other and run our businesses and systems. There is an accelerated change in how we consume goods, manage ourselves and set moral and ethical standards for each other.

At this time, understanding teamwork and its' role is critical for leaders.

Build to Outperform has practical, easy to implement strategies to identify, develop, engage and reward high performing teams based on his experiences as a CHRO Executive, Board Director, and Executive Coach to CEOs and C suite leaders.

This book reflects guiding principles which we share in common vision which would help all organizations build a global community of leaders who create shareholder value through high performing teams.

John Mattone
Bestselling Author and the World's Top Executive Coach

INTRODUCTION

"A story has no beginning or end: arbitrarily, one chooses that moment of experience from which to look back or from which to look ahead."

— Graham Greene

In my 30 years of experience, with a professional background as an ex-CHRO and then executive and independent board director for large and mid-sized organizations, I have worked with and led large, diverse teams and driven high-growth businesses in Asia as well as globally. I have been a part of eight mergers and acquisitions during my career.

I have made strategies and am now advising organizations on how to achieve high growth through organic and inorganic growth. Currently, I'm an executive coach and independent director, executive coach to over 100 C suite leaders. And I worked with them to ensure the implementation of a strategy to execution, driving high growth, handling mergers and acquisitions. From a people perspective, organization design, restructuring, and change management help build an inspirational leadership style. I have the credibility of coaching more than 100 C suite leaders across global multinational corporations, large global Indian corporates, family-run businesses, and public sector undertakings. Including all of these areas and the number of researches that we have done on different organizations. I've reached an understanding that high-performing organizations are not buried by a great analysis of numbers or a great presentation of numbers.

The right way to gauge the success and, even more so, the organization's potential depends on whether they are built by having a clear strategy in place, having the right organizational structure, and whether they have the right operating model. How does this organization define the right product, processes, which enable success? Most importantly, do they allow and practice a culture of high performance and high performing teams? Because even if you get your strategy, structure, and products right and are not complemented with a high-performing team, it will not achieve its vision or a sense of purpose.

The research that I have done on various organizations has stated repeatedly that one of the key reasons organizations don't achieve their goals is because they don't have pockets of consistent performance across all teams. 55% of organizations globally have attributed not having high-performing teams consistently or constant high-performance levels as one of the key reasons.

In organizations that aren't able to drive high performance, it was also noted that there was a lack of consistency in raising the bar of performance, the interdependence of goals, the lack of cultural compatibility, and imposing standards. Other problems include not being aware of the cultural nuances, not investing enough in training and development, not setting up leadership pipelines, and more. All of these are problems worth addressing.

This book addresses all of these issues that aren't spoken about enough to date. How do we build high-performing teams such that the organization can achieve its mission, vision, purpose? How to ensure that strategy turns into execution seamlessly? This book is not about just achieving your targets. But about building sustainable, high performance consistently. It's not a quick fix way of solving your immediate problems, but it's about a sustainable performance for businesses, whether in the short term, medium-term or long term. This book is carefully crafted to help you identify the gaps and challenges in building high-performance teams in terms of analysis, strategies, execution, and sustaining your team. It will also equip you with the tools and techniques for attracting talent, high-performing talent, retaining talent, developing talent, and engaging talent. It is all about understanding. Why is it important to be in high-performing teams? Why is it important to have one? If you've never thought about this, now is the time. It is high time to start bridging those gaps that come your way of building high-performing teams and navigating those gaps.

It's about building high-performing teams focusing on hiring the right kind of people, developing and retaining the right talent, creating a culture of trust and collaboration, high accountability, and determining the best ways of rewarding and maintaining high performance. All I would like to say while you get ready to start your ride here is, you've chosen a wonderful journey for yourselves and, more importantly, for your team and the future of each one of your organizations. However, this isn't a journey that is a quick one. This book isn't about reaching the destination, but it is more about how to make your trip a safe, easy, and memorable one.

Let's begin.

PART A:
SETTING UP HIGH PERFORMING TEAMS

1

WHY SHOULD WE CREATE HIGH PERFORMING TEAMS?

"That's one small step for man, one giant leap for mankind."- Neil Armstrong.

20th July 1969, the whole world listened to a statement that shall perhaps remain the most motivating one for the whole of mankind. Neil Armstrong said the above quoted words as he set humanity's first step on the Moon. Today we remember him as the face of the Apollo 11 mission. The more well-informed ones would also not forget Buzz Aldrin, the second man to set foot on the Moon, and Michael Collins, who flew the Columbia crew module while his two crewmates landed the lunar lander Eagle on the Moon. However, they would just be the faces of the Apollo 11 mission.

The entire project would only succeed because the team did thorough research and testing to ensure its successful outcome. Mankind may have landed on the Moon in 1969; however, the endeavor had started long before that iconic day. It was a national goal set by President John F Kennedy in 1961.

He was very clear in his objective when he said that America had to land a man on the Moon and return him safely to Earth within a decade. National Aeronautics and Space Association (NASA) would roll the ball in a space race to reach the Moon. The Apollo 11 mission began two years prior, in 1967. Even the landing destination was exhaustively studied, with mission planners poring over various data, including the geography of the surface, to find the safest spot.

Moreover, the three men who would fly into space for this momentous occasion would undergo rigorous training to fly to the Moon. Countless analysts, engineers, and technicians believed in that dream set forth by Kennedy and worked hard to put humanity on the Moon. It is one of the best examples of Mission Accomplished from the pages of history.

So, what can we learn from one of the greatest feats in human history? Success can be achieved when you have a clear mission and structure in place. One crucial element of a structure is the team. For the three astronauts to achieve success, many more people worked tirelessly. This lesson also translates across to the business sector. Let me pose this question: What do you think is the current challenge faced by businesses in terms of consistency, delivery, and converting strategies into action? Any perusal of successful companies and even failed businesses points toward either clarity regarding objectives or the organizational structure.

One of the key things that I have experienced during my tenure as a C-suite leader and a board-level advisor can be stated as follows: The key to a covert strategy to execution is a clear plan; checks, balances, and the right strategy. Most importantly, a high-performing team needs to consistently align its objectives and outperform.

When Kennedy declared the goal to put a man on the Moon, the objective was relevant. It was the era of the Cold War, and the USA and USSR were stuck in a space race. Then one needs the right organizational structure, operating model, right people, and the right culture to deliver the strategic plan. The USA had NASA, which set a goal and worked toward it. The next important element is the right process, infrastructure, tools, technology, teams, and culture. NASA was staffed with people who wanted to achieve that goal.

Let us examine these elements.

The first issue I would like to examine is the importance of strategy. Look at some of the big business giants over the past 50 years. How many of them hold the same market leadership position? If I were to bring up digital cameras, what are the companies that come to your mind? Sony, Canon, and Nikon would be the obvious names. How about Kodak? If you know your cameras' history, you will see that Kodak first patented the digital camera in the 1970s. But they did not realize that they had the chance to lead the market. They were the market leaders in film-based photography. They were also making a lot of revenue by selling the film rolls for the cameras. When one of their engineers invented the digital camera, the company adopted the wrong strategy. Their product was weighed down by flaws like excessive weight, low resolution, and prolonged processing time. They did not focus on improving the product. Instead, they decided to stay put. Kodak's competitors did not stay put. This strategy would lead to Kodak filing for bankruptcy in 2012.

Another example I would like to illustrate is that of Nokia. In the 1970s, they operated in many industries like TV production, gas masks, paper manufacturing, and even plastics and chemicals. But in the early 1970s, they invented a new digital switch for telephone exchanges, which was the first step in Nokia revolutionizing communication technology, specifically cellular communication technology. They were already the pioneers of the 1G technology, which shifted communication using radio waves to analog signals. In the 1980s, they would bring out products like the Mobira Senator, Mobira Talkman, and Mobira Cityman, predecessors of the mobile phone. They would further revolutionize communication technology by bringing the 2G GSM network, which shifted to digital signals.

In the 90s, they decided to focus on cellular communication, leading to the launch of the Nokia 2100 in 1994. However, they severely underestimated the demand. They could not keep up with the demand for the Nokia 2100. They realized that there was an issue in their supply chain. They were relying on a Japanese company for building their technology. So, they decided to learn how to make it themselves and become the name in mobile phones. By 2008, they had close to half the market share in mobile phones. Then it changed. Steve Jobs introduced the world to the iPhone. Soon Google would join Apple, and the way we used mobile phones changed. Nokia simply could not keep up. Nokia did not keep up with the strategy, and it almost threw them out of the sole leadership.

While the market demanded Android and iOS software, Nokia stuck to the Symbian software. Nokia fell from grace and was close to filing for bankruptcy before Microsoft bought them out.

The next element I would like to highlight is the right organizational structure. When we speak of organizational structure, I have to talk about teams. In my experience, the most difficult element of those aforementioned has a good team. Teams are purely internally driven. The best of strategies, the best of processes, and the best of technology will not give results if there is no good team. We have seen several organizations with great strategies, great processes, and great technology and fail to deliver because the team had not updated. The teams could not envision what could be done, so they could not perform well. The teams could not cope with the current trends.

In the year 1999, the second most-used search engine was Excite. However, it was a distant second to Yahoo. At this point, a person named Larry Page approached Excite with an offer to acquire his company, which was called Google. They negotiated a $750,000 deal with a 1% stake in Excite. However, the negotiations would fall due to one singular demand. Page specified that if Google were to be acquired by Excite, Excite would have to discard their existing search technologies and adopt only Google's technologies. In the end, Excite's CEO George Bell declined as he believed in his team more than in Page's team. Google had built on the trend of serving ads based on search terms started by the search site GoTo.com. They made on that trend to become the behemoth they are today.

Another case would be that of Blockbuster. It was once the undisputed king of the video-rental industry. It was a brick-and-mortar company in over 2800 locations worldwide within twelve years of its inception. At this time, Reed Hastings and Marc Randolph started a Netflix company. They began with a video-rental-by-mail service. They created an online division as well. Three years later, in 2000, they approached Blockbuster to see if they could work together. They wanted $50 million for the acquisition of Netflix and offered to run the online division for Blockbuster. Hastings would later recall that they were laughed out of the building. Blockbuster failed to notice the trend, and by the time they launched an online platform four years later, Netflix was too far ahead for them to catch up.

Twenty years from that eventful day in 2000, Netflix would be valued at $203 billion. But how can teams be more effective? They have to be sharp to stay relevant. Teams need to relook at the way they define their goals.

They need to constantly review the set performance standards: how they evaluate performance and how they keep developing and reinventing themselves. A highly effective team will continuously innovate and find new and better ways of doing things. Look at the case of Oldsmobile. In the fifties and sixties, Oldsmobile produced the cars of the day. They were glamorous in style and a marvel in engineering.

They had perfected the idea of art and science when it came to car making. Oldsmobile would be the first to introduce many common features of cars today: gasoline-powered engines, chrome-plated trims, fully automatic transmission, front-wheel drive, and even airbags. They were innovative in their car designs. It was a company with a rich history founded in 1897. It was also a part of General Motors, a giant in the auto industry. However, GM would fold the company down in 2004.

Why? Their teams stopped innovating. They did not look to upgrade or improve their engines. Their car designs were no longer unique and seemed to be more like other GM cars. The teams at Oldsmobile failed to reevaluate and innovate and therefore failed. Another way teams can be effective is when they have diversity. Diversity ensures that a team is exposed to different perspectives and viewpoints. People from different cultures will perceive situations differently. Good teams will look to encourage and enable such diverse views. A study conducted by the Harvard Business Review found that diverse teams could solve problems quicker than non-diverse teams. The study emphasizes the importance of diversity in the new age where we face uncertain and complex changes.

It is about managing different cultures and thought processes, managing people with different skills and backgrounds, and contributing to evolution. If we were to look at the world of sports, look at the 2018 FIFA World Cup winners or the 2019 Cricket World Cup winners. Fifteen of the twenty-three-man squad of France's 2018 World Cup-winning team were of African descent, and 21 of the 23 came from immigrant families.

England's captain Eoin Morgan said this of his 2019 World Cup-winning team, "… everyone's standards rose. If anything, the mood around the camp did too. Multiculturalism made us stronger." So how do you make teams function better? You have to include them and empower them in the decision-making processes. Trust and responsibility will make your teams perform better. Let us take the example of the Airline industry. Say a person checks in and then asks for a seat upgrade.

You will notice that the airline staff manning the counter is empowered to give you an upgrade. They can make this decision without having it approved by a chain of command. Just imagine if such a process was limited by red tape. The amount of time it would take would surely lead to customer dissatisfaction. Hence, it is vital that teams be agile and empowered in decision-making processes that can shape the future of the company.

It is especially true in this technological day. The challenges are complex, and people can no longer be as effective if they are married to the assembly line production model. They have to be problem solvers. Teams, too, cannot simply be just a function-oriented entity. They will have to carry out their designated functions and respond to many demands and pitch in at emergencies as and when needed.

Technology has changed the way we work. The world is far more dynamic and requires people and teams to be increasingly virtual, agile, flexible, and empowered. The brick-and-mortar base of centralized operations is like a relic of the past. Communication can be accomplished quickly via applications like Microsoft Teams and Slack. There could be occasions where managers may not even see their teams on a daily basis. This has become true after the pandemic.

Many tech-based companies actually grew during the COVID pandemic. As lockdowns were announced, companies let their staff work from home, which led to a rise in Zoom usage by 326% in the year 2020. Similarly, the cloud database company Snowflake's revenues increased by 124% in the same year. It was not just the offices that were closed due to the lockdown. The online fitness company Peloton saw its revenues rise by 139%. The greatest turnaround perhaps could be seen in the food delivery company, DoorDash. It was operating at a loss of $616 million on revenue of $885 million in 2019. After the pandemic struck, its revenues increased to $2.89 billion in 2020.

CASE STUDY:

I would like to bring to your attention the particular case of a large garment retail organization. It also happened to be a market leader. I happened to be working there at a very senior executive level. The company boasted of excellent products and good market credibility and was an innovative thinker ahead of its time. However, it did not have consistent high-performing teams. They had good sales and marketing teams.

These teams would strike deals that ended up doing big business. But the production team could not keep the costs under control. This inability to bring down costs eroded the EBITDA (Earnings Before Interest, Taxes, Depreciation, and Amortization.) On reflection, I could see that the company could not retain high-performing teams. There was no process in place by which they could identify and hire the right kind of people.

The strategies were not clear or clearly communicated. The finance department did not feature a robust MIS process, picking up financial triggers early and addressing them. So, here was an organization with a great product and a visionary leader at the top. Despite having these advantages, the company could not produce sustained profits and started to incur losses. Even if under-performing team members were identified, no steps were taken to enhance or hone their skills. They were instead shifted to different departments.

The emphasis should have been on improvement rather than on rearrangement. Such actions only contributed toward a toxic culture that did not impress upon improvement. So instead of addressing the problem, it was just transferred elsewhere.

The right approach, in this case, would have been as follows:
- Set clear goals
- Evaluate performances regularly
- Review performances regularly
- Develop people in the right areas
- Address deficiencies in skills by putting them through performance-improvement plans

There were rewards and recognitions which differentiated high performers and underperformers. High-performing teams were given regular increments and were always encouraged and rewarded. Under-performing teams were not rewarded. Creating this differentiated reward strategy was important and critical.

When I was tasked with coming up with a solution to the issue, I drew up a three-point plan. I first emphasized the need for a clear strategy from the top. The second point was that this particular strategy had to be communicated downwards in clear and concise ways. The third point was about performance.

I identified four crucial components within performance in terms of financial and operating results like EBITDA, PAT (Profit After Tax).
- Revenue Growth, New client acquisition, client retention ratio.
- Compliance and process improvement.
- People development.
- Learning and growth.

If you were to observe clearly, you would notice that all these four pillars of performance are measured and linked to the business strategy, departmental/functional goals, and team goals, and subsequently to individual goals. Therefore, it starts with the head of business drawing up strategic goals. If we were to return to the moon landing, Kennedy would have fulfilled this role. Based on the strategic goals determined by the business head, the function or department heads would then come up with the roadmap to achieve that goal. NASA department heads would have functioned under their own roadmaps to help put the man on the Moon. Then you would have the performance of individual team members, which was then correlated with different teams.

The performance will improve when there is a clear structure and flow to an organization and its strategy. Even members of the team who initially seemed to be concerned only about their individual performance will soon start to also focus on the team's performance as their individual performance is closely related to the group's performance. Such an environment would only nurture a culture of collaboration. When there is a strong culture of collaboration, high-performing teams are born and thrive.

We affected some changes in the organization mentioned above based on my recommendations. We allocated the average increment and bonus for high-performing teams three to five times. Those who did not perform were given lesser responsibilities. We made it clear that high-performing teams would be recognized and rewarded. We introduced a recognition program where people were recognized on a monthly, quarterly, and yearly basis. We also gave out different awards [Gold, Platinum, and Silver Awards.]

We propagated the idea that individual performance was linked to the team's performance, and it was an essential cog rather than a separate element by itself. As a result, the organization's revenue grew by 18% in one year, and EBITDA had increased by 35%. 8% of underperformers were separated, while 35% of the employees turned around their performances.

TAKEAWAYS:

- Have a clear strategy that is specific, measurable, attainable, and time-bound.
- Ensure that the strategy is communicated effectively top-down, right from the business functional heads to managers and first-time managers and individual contributors. Everybody should be able to see how their efforts contribute toward the accomplishment of the company's strategic goals.
- Create clear measures of performance. Define what constitutes a good performance, and contrastingly, what constitutes an ineffective performance. Relate effective performance to rewards and underperformance to consequences. Give fair opportunities and timely feedback. Ensure that people are given sufficient development opportunities (training, coaching, and mentoring). They should also be provided with adequate time to turn around their performance.
  If there are no improvements despite such efforts, take decisive action. When you identify an ineffective performer, determine if it is a skill or a will issue. Skills can be built and developed via external means but demand internal commitment and cannot be resolved easily by training or coaching.
- It was found that 8% of the underperformers had to leave the organization. We followed the development process. However, there were no positive results. What is the moral of this story? Take decisive actions when it is necessary. In this case, they let go of the consistent underperformers.
  In their absence, the company could go out and identify the right talent and build high-performing teams.
- There should be rewards to high performers and consequences to underperformers.
- Set very clear goals. Link those goals to strategies.
- Ensure goals align with the business strategies, and there is an inter-dependence of goals between various departments. Ensure that there is a focus on collaboration.
- Ensure that there is an element of team dependency on goals. Ensure there is a clear system of rewards and consequences, which is linked to performance. Reward right behaviors.

Focus continuously on training, coaching, developing, and mentoring. Set extended goals for the team, which inspire the team to work better and celebrate success.

HOW DOES THE ORGANIZATION SUFFER IF THEY DO NOT HAVE HIGH-PERFORMING INDIVIDUALS AND TEAMS?

- There is a direct impact on the numbers of the organization and performance, which includes revenues, profits, and retention of high performers.
- It impacts innovation in the organization. It erodes team motivation and demotivates the high performers.
- Tolerating underperformers for too long and not rewarding high performers gives rise to mediocrity in the organization.
- It is important to ensure that high-performing teams are rewarded and retained. This will help attract the right kind of talent.

2

CHALLENGES IN CREATING HIGH PERFORMING TEAMS.

"Great organizations are not built by brilliant individuals. They are built by average individuals performing brilliantly".

- Ajay Bakshi.

One of the more shocking news in professional sports in 2021 has been the departure of Lionel Messi from Barcelona. The Spanish club could not register the player for the new season due to the rules in place. I find this incident fascinating because of the events that precipitated this departure. The disruption started in 2017. Just two years before this eventful date, Barcelona was among the better-run football clubs in the world. They had one of the most fearsome attacking tridents in Messi, Neymar, and Suarez. However, in 2017, Paris Saint-Germain paid over 200 million euros to prize Neymar away from Barcelona. Barcelona had been a juggernaut when it came to commercial revenues. They also arguably had one of the best high-performing teams in the world.

But Neymar's departure was the fall of the first domino.

They now had the opportunity to plan and replace Neymar and work toward transitioning their aging side to a younger side still capable of mounting title challenges. But Barcelona went a different route. They went on to sign a promising young talent in Ousmane Dembele and a precocious superstar in Phillipe Coutinho. They used all the money they received for Neymar on these two players. However, two players thrived in the same position on the pitch. Coutinho's other strength came from his free-roaming role. However, Barcelona already possessed someone far superior in that role in Lionel Messi. Barcelona only aggravated the issue by agreeing to massive salary packages with these players. So, when these players struggled, they could not move them as no other club was willing to match their salaries. This problem manifested onto the pitch, where they struggled to remain competitive. They could field a team filled with players who were superstars in their own right. But they had no real coherence as a fluid and tactically astute team. Barcelona's answer was to sign another aging superstar in Antoine Griezmann on another expensive pay package.

They had repeated the same mistake. Griezmann was a superstar but played in the same positions as Messi. Soon, as 2021 would reveal, Barcelona had too many players on too much money – they were paying salaries well over what they made in revenues. As a consequence, as we saw in 2021, Messi would depart to join Paris Saint-Germain.

While there are many lessons about financial prudence and management, from my perspective, I see the issue as talent identification. Sports teams, especially at the elite level, are the literal definition of high-performing teams. The challenge of spotting and grooming the right talent is crucial. If you fail, you will be left with expensive mistakes like Barcelona, which you will find hard to shift.

The idea that you need to find the right talent translates to every professional domain. On a quick side note, Liverpool, one of the beneficiaries of Barcelona's splurge when they sold Coutinho, would show how to build a high-performing team. Liverpool possessed a famed attacking triumvirate of their own. However, their midfield and defense were considered to be holding the side back.

When they sold Coutinho, they identified that these areas needed addressing. So, with the money they obtained by selling Coutinho, they bought three transformative players.

Virgil van Dijk was a commanding center-half, Alisson Becker was one of the best sweeper-keepers in the world, and Fabinho was one of the elite ball-winning defensive midfielders. Unlike what happened with Barcelona, these players fit within the tactical set-up of the team. Extensive scouting was done on their characters and mentality. The three players would become the spine of one of the most feared sides in the world as they won the Champions League, Premier League, and other trophies. When you do not bring in the right talent, you have every chance to tumble down like Barcelona. So, what are the challenges you will face when you want to assemble a high-performing team?

The first challenge you will face when it comes to assembling a high-performing team is the availability of the right talent. You need to get the right people at the right time and at the right cost. When you compromise on talent, you compromise on performance.

For example, let us say you find a person with the right technical requisites. They are well versed when it comes to organizational needs, but they do not possess the right mindset. Such a person will never give you their 100% or be willing to go the extra mile to deliver the best product. They may find it easier to coast along. On the contrary, let us say you find another person who may be a 70% fit for the technical needs. They may not have the right amount of experience but is demonstrably a learner and has the fire in the belly to go the extra mile. You can see that this person wishes to learn and not only displays a can-do attitude but is also a team player. Such a candidate is the perfect candidate.

In a study published by the Harvard Business Review, Peter Cappelli explores how hiring practices and approaches have gone wrong. He talks of how many resources are wasted in identifying and hiring passive candidates. He talks of how HR professionals look to identify experienced personnel from other companies.

It means their motivation to move comes from money rather than ambition. He also cites other research to demonstrate how companies, on average, only fill 11% of their vacancies with individually targeted people. So, what are the essential elements in building a high-performing team? From my experience, I have boiled it down to these four:
1. Getting the right people at the right cost.
2. Developing the right kind of leaders.
3. Creating the right kind of career opportunities.

4. Retaining talented individuals.

Let us explore these elements together.

I already have stressed the importance of hiring the right people at the right cost with the example of Barcelona. However, how would you look to identify the right talent? Peter Cappelli looks at two obvious flaws when it comes to the hiring process.

The first flaw he identifies is the usage of third parties by means of outsourcing the hiring process. The second mistake that he calls out is the dependence on referrals. He clearly underlines this when he cites research to show that referrals only work when the referee brings the referred under their wing.

Otherwise, the productivity of the referral system is not that high. So, what should you look for in a candidate? The obvious criteria would be the right technical skills, the right professional competence, and the right kind of experience. However, one should also look for some of the softer skills like learning agility, cultural adaptivity, working in different environments, collaborative ways of working, and being an effective team player. You will find that getting the right mix of all these categories is difficult. You will rarely find candidates who tick every single box.

So, it is up to you to find how these candidates fit within the group dynamic. How do they complement the current team? This idea leads into the element of leadership. You need the right kind of leader to identify the gaps and strategize accordingly.

One of the perennial concerns, be it in corporate, educational, political, or social organizations or in the sports arena, is about having the right leaders. Several people have asked me a key question: "Are leaders born, or are they made?"

My response to that is to quote Field Marshal Sam Manekshaw:

"Leaders are made, not necessarily born."

Leadership is a trait or a skill that can be developed in people; no one is born with those skills. Even if some people are born with a legacy of leadership, the chances are high that they may not necessarily make great leaders. One of the key challenges here is developing the right kind of leadership skills, which will eventually create high-performing teams.

WHY ARE LEADERS IMPORTANT TO BUILD A HIGH-PERFORMING TEAM?

As I mentioned earlier, a leader is necessary to spot the right talent who will be the best fit within the team and produce the best in their jobs. You may wonder how a leader can contribute to the success of a high-performing team. Leaders are essential to create the right environment and work culture that facilitates the team to function better. They will ensure that there is always an open line of communication and an environment that fosters trust and collaboration.

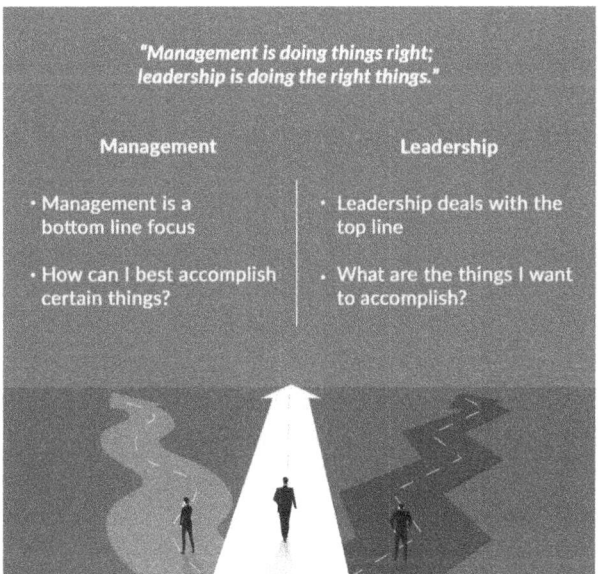

Leaders play a pivotal role in ensuring implementing strategy to execution. You need leaders who can lead by example in a high-performing team. They will be the driving force of change and innovation by constantly assessing and reviewing processes to enhance efficiency without compromising on effectiveness. They will also look to the people around them to help them in this goal. They will look to encourage promotions from within and give the space to the employees to showcase their abilities. They will trust them by granting them privileges and responsibilities. A study by Deloitte in 2020 revealed that around 86% of the employees leave their jobs due to a shortage of career-developmental opportunities.

You need good leaders to chart the way and show how there are opportunities for growth within the organization. If you were to question me on what exactly a team needs to evolve into a high-performance team, my answer would be that you need a clear objective and effective communication to all the stakeholders involved. Leaders come to the fore on these occasions. They will ensure that the objective is communicated clearly and then formulate the strategy for achieving the said objective. As I indicated before, they will formulate the strategy by involving all the team members. They will set out their short-term and medium-term goals and, in a collaborative effort, draw up the roadmap to achieve these goals. Leaders will stress the values of the organization but will not be trapped by any hierarchical or bureaucratic hurdles which will affect team performance. Leaders will also recognize the efforts of the team to keep them motivated and feel valued.

HOW DOES EFFECTIVE LEADERSHIP AFFECT A TEAM?

The foremost benefit will be seen in the morale and camaraderie of the team members. Due to the collaborative work culture, they will feel valued and recognize themselves as key cogs within the organization. They will start to enjoy working for the company. As they are exposed to opportunities to develop and hone their skills, they will grow and contribute to the continued growth and prosperity of the company. When employees feel valued, there will also be a lesser rate of employee turnover. When the employee turnover rate falls, you will also find that retaining your best talent will be easier.

However, the greatest benefit a leader brings to a high-performing team is the clarity and understanding of the roles within the team and how they contribute to the objectives and its accomplishment.

Specifically, leaders are needed to instill a sense of mutual respect and belief. When leaders encourage collaborative work cultures, they not only instill their own beliefs and trust but also signal to the team that the people within it are talented and capable.

The leader will be able to pinpoint where they can complement one another's efforts and fill in any possible weaknesses. They also instill confidence within the team. As leaders assume the role of facilitators, they empower the team to be confident in their abilities and capabilities. By presenting growth opportunities, the leader enables the team members to become more confident with time.

However, it is not just in these areas that leaders develop high-performing teams. They will identify aspects within the team members who need development and training. They will be looking to enhance the expertise and talent of the team members by organizing training programs and skill-development exercises.

I would also like to caution you that when leaders present their team members with responsibilities and opportunities, it does not mean that they have no control. Even as they grant these opportunities, they also establish clear boundaries for the team. They will do so with adequate communication. They will ensure that the team members are provided the correct information on achieving their objectives. In a similar vein, they will also monitor the work done and provide valuable feedback to the team members. They will identify areas of improvement and assess the strengths and weaknesses within the team and share them with the team members. The leadership role evolves with the development of the high-performing teams. During the initial stages, you want the leader to assume an authoritarian position. As the team members find their footing and their roles within the team, the leader needs to be the one who provides directions by issuing instructions and guides the members through the teething phase.

However, once the team reaches a stage of maturity and comfort, the leader will then have to discard the authoritarian role and be more of a team mentor and facilitate the collaborative work culture that I mentioned before. So how do you guarantee the right career opportunities for your employees? You can only provide opportunities to your employees when you know the extent of their capability.

To build their capabilities, you need to ensure that employees take time off and focus on personal development. They will also need to devote sufficient time for rejuvenation. However, I am not suggesting they leave their day jobs and only focus on development. However, employees definitely need adequate time to recharge and reflect. This is important to retain high-performing teams.

Right interventions must be planned.

I think the right intervention starts by identifying the right kind of developmental needs. You need to look for things that can be done to help an employee improve his performance. Some of the questions that you could ask are as follows: How does the employee apply their knowledge to the job, be it academic knowledge through certifications, or reading books, etc.?

What are some of the challenges the employees face, and how do they navigate through these challenges? How can their developmental needs, especially some of the softer skills, be honed? How do they collaborate? How do they handle conflicts? How do they influence others, especially in areas where they do not have the authority?

How can they communicate their ideas with clarity, conviction, and enthusiasm, and how would they listen effectively? How do they demonstrate empathy? How would they demonstrate emotional intelligence? How would they create a common sense of purpose and ensure that everyone works toward a common goal?

With a limited pool of talent, there is a war for talent acquisition. These people are in demand outside as well as inside the office. I have seen managers tending to hold employees back. But when you give time to employees to develop themselves, you will find that you will be able to provide them with the right kind of opportunities.

When you focus on these elements, you will find that the fourth element of retaining the right talent will be easier when it comes to the war for talent. When high-performing individuals feel valued and are provided with enough career growth opportunities, they will more than likely stay with you. So, what are some of the key ingredients and challenges in creating high-performing teams?

One of the key challenges in creating high-performing teams is the process of performance management. There should be a review of the goals of the high-performing teams. Are the goals identified clearly? Are they joined together? Are they aligned upward? How are individual goals linked with the organization's goals? Are the goals cascading down to people, right from the top management? How are those goals aligned cross-functionally (horizontally)? How are they connected to various other teams and other departments?

The idea is that individual performance matters as they contribute to the performance of the entire team. How will their performance help the team? This alignment has to be seen very clearly. On the other hand, if they are not doing their jobs effectively, how is that going to impact the team's performance? For instance, if a person, let's say, Jack, is not doing his job well, does he realize that he is also bringing down the entire team's performance? When it is teamwork, everyone's performance is aligned with each other.

The next challenge is that of goal setting and setting performance standards. You need these standards to help people perform better and also aid in the process of providing proper and timely feedback. Different organizations have different processes of performance management, whether it is a social organization or a political organization.

While some carry this out formally, many do it informally. Those who do it formally have a biannual appraisal process or an annual appraisal process. Many public sector enterprises or state-run organizations have adopted such models wherein employees are assessed both by internal assessors and external assessors. Here, the employee's performance, potential, and capability to manage the promotion are measured.

This brings me to the next question.

HOW SHOULD PERFORMANCE STANDARDS BE SET?

Performance must be measured not just on keyboard performance indicators or your key result areas but also on the softer skills. Employees should not just be focused on short-term results and must also consider long-term results. So, the question that naturally springs from this perspective is why is potential not given much weightage when it comes to measuring individual performance.

It is especially critical when you consider that potential is given a lot of weightage while promoting employees and identifying people who are capable of managing bigger individual roles. The simple answer is that potential is about identifying a person's inherent capabilities to do a job, which they have not done before. You cannot measure performance with potential because that would not encourage productivity in high-performing teams. We shall discuss performance assessment later.

Let us first discuss the ways by which you can measure potential. It may seem tricky. But there are different ways to do it. There are structured ways of measuring potential through assessments. One way would be to do a survey where people of different backgrounds assess employees and rate them. You could also leverage multiple tools like psychometrics, business simulations, role-plays, etc.

When it comes to role-plays, the employees are put in different situations, and their reactions are measured. This method can assess an employee's capability in unfamiliar situations.

When a person is put through unfamiliar situations, how do they react to them? How do they think, and what kind of decisions are they going to make? What could be the impact of some of these decisions? How does a person plan? A lot of similar traits are measured. This is a very effective way of assessing potential in people.

Another key challenge in high-performing teams is feedback. Employees need feedback to motivate or correct themselves. You may ask if there is an appropriate way of sharing feedback. In my opinion, the most important element in feedback is its timeliness. Feedback must be shared as and when possible. Managers must not wait for an appraisal process. If you share feedback before the appraisal process, it actually becomes feedforward. You provide feedback because you want to help people improve their performance. Giving feedback after the appraisal process is just a post-mortem process, where you are only assessing what went well and what went wrong. It would be 'feedforward' for next year. By giving proper feedback before the appraisal process, you help the employee take corrective actions at the right time.

Here are a few tips while giving feedback:

- Make it soon after the event.
- Tell people what they have done well and what they can do better.
- Help them identify their blind spots by asking them reflective questions. If they are not able to self-reflect, then give them the data and various examples and instances.

Feedforward helps create self-awareness in people about their areas that need improvement (individual and team), but it also ensures that they can address those concerns.

Feedforward helps them think through what can be done to address the grey areas. 70-20-10 model. Feedback aids in self-reflection, which goes a long way in the development of the team members. Hence, it is crucial that leaders embrace this role of being a coach/mentor who can give feedback to their teammates at every step. The company must also sponsor the employees for pursuing relevant courses, be it technical courses, functional courses, behavioral courses, or leadership courses, or anything else which can aid in their development. All of these interventions should be linked to their developmental needs and their career aspirations, which could be immediate as well as futuristic.

The other important part when developing a team is ensuring that the employees are given sufficient opportunities to apply what they have learned. Suppose you send an individual contributor to complete a course on strategy from one of the leading business schools.

It would be a wasted effort if the contributor were not in a position to apply the learnings on the job. It would be like providing a person the wrong medicine for the wrong ailment.

Maybe a particular individual needs to focus more on technical skills, collaboration, or building collaborative skills, or maybe they need to focus on improving their client conversation techniques. The individual's needs must be taken into account. Giving the right prescription to the right person is important. Otherwise, the entire exercise makes no sense. This is another major challenge that I have often witnessed.: The right kind of development inputs are not given to the right individuals.

Another area that I feel needs attention is presenting employees with the opportunity to practice, develop, and hone their skills regularly. There is a saying: "Rome was not built in a day." Skill development, too, does not happen overnight. It is all about repetition and practice. The more you do it, the better you become. If you were to observe any high-performing team in the sport, you would see the emphasis they place on repetitions during training or practice. A lot of skills can be developed, which includes the skill of creating high-performing teams.

So, resilience and continuous feedback are ways of developing skills. Let us talk a bit about performance now: What differentiates winners from losers? The first point of difference comes from the knowledge of the job. Such knowledge is not something that can be built or acquired overnight. It comes with a lot of painstaking effort and training. One needs to invest in taking the right courses and keep applying the learning from such courses on the job. As mentioned before, one also needs to continuously self-reflect and take feedback on what is working and what is not. Good teams do that consistently. Winners do that consistently.

Secondly, winners do not allow failures to impact them. They learn from failure, take the learning, improvise it, and move ahead. They always emerge successfully after a failure, be it in sports arenas, the political arena, or any other business. Of course, not every match can be won. But winners do not let one failure bring their spirits down. Instead, they will reflect on what can be learned from their failures.

They will evaluate areas that need improvement and work on them. Michael Jordan, considered one of the greatest players to have ever played the game of basketball, once remarked, "I have missed more than 9,000 shots in my career. I have lost almost 300 games. On 26 occasions, I have been entrusted to take the game-winning shot, and I missed. I have failed over and over and over again in my life. And that is why I succeed". He learned from those failures and would become one of the iconic players of the sport. Similarly, if someone fails, they need to ask themselves, "How do I ensure that I do not repeat the same mistakes?". How can one improve? This is where winners differ from losers. It is the continuous process of learning and not allowing failures to put you down.

Thirdly, winners (individual and team) have a can-do approach. They believe they are capable of achieving the impossible, and they dream big. They help one another by standing and protecting one another. When things go wrong, they do not get caught up in blame games. Winning teams try to leverage their strengths. They do not talk much; they let their work showcase their capabilities.

All team members in a winning team are generally in agreement, and although they are dependent on each other, their individual capacities are equal. Everyone on the team is equally equipped. For instance, when one of the team members does not perform well for some reason in a particular match, a particular event, or even in a particular client meeting, winners do not panic. Someone else on the team steps up and takes over. All the members on the team have skills that complement each other, and this is what gives rise to diversity. This diversity in skills is what builds high-performing teams:

The team can have one person who is brilliant in planning, another person who is good at execution, and yet another person who is very good at backend operations. All these skills complement each other. Thus, these high-performing teams can take on any kind of task. That said, it is important to make sure this diversity contributes to the smooth and seamless functioning of the team.

Another factor that differentiates winners and losers is that winning teams keep reviewing their processes regularly and look for ways to better themselves every day. They always look at reinventing themselves and readapting to the environment. For instance, let us say there is a team that might have performed brilliantly pre-COVID.

However, with the ongoing pandemic, this team is incurring huge losses since every meeting became virtual. Perhaps the team's unique strengths and charisma do not translate well across a digital screen. The team will fail when they are not able to adapt, and the employees are not flexible enough. Therefore, the team, including the managers, needs to be agile and continuously reinvent themselves. The team members must also keep scanning their environment, work-wise. They need to be aware of what is happening around them, and they need to keep themselves up-to-date. What is the competitor planning? In which direction are the consumer preferences tilting? Another important element in high-performing teams is that all members must be empowered to make decisions.

Every team member must be able to make decisions and take final calls in the work they do. Taking initiatives is crucial in creating high-performing teams. Winners always take the initiative; they wait for no one. They do not wait to be told what needs to be done. Winners practice lateral thinking and search for different ways to solve a problem. This attitude drives innovation. Winners are not satisfied with the status quo. They always want to do more. They shake themselves out of their comfort zone and always set challenging targets before them. Keeping this attitude is important because even though not every target may be met when you aspire for more, you are closer to achieving your goals, thereby bettering your performance at every given opportunity.

Winners and high-performing teams are passionate. They always go the extra mile, and this extra effort is not only for the monetary benefits. When money becomes your sole motivation, you will burn out after a while. The enthusiasm and passion which drive winning teams cannot be substituted by financial rewards. Winners motivate each other, professionally and personally. That said, they respect each other's boundaries. They address conflicts and hurdles. There is no place for miscommunication. In fact, disagreements are seen as an alternate thought process that needs introspection. Winners look at conflicts positively and constructively. They do not take it as a personal criticism. However, losers do the exact opposite.

Winners take stretched targets, and they are continuously looking at improving themselves; they are never satisfied with the status quo. They always try to innovate and come out with newer ideas and solutions.

They look for methods to do their work quicker and faster in the most cost-effective way. They keep challenging each other.

Losers, meanwhile, are happy with a little success. They wait for orders rather than take initiatives of their own and are very happy with the status quo. Winners are also willing to collaborate. Speaking of collaboration, there is an inherent difference between competition and collaboration. Healthy competition is where people challenge each other and are willing to collaborate and achieve common team goals.

Finally, winners celebrate success. Celebrating success is a very positive way of reinforcing the core messages. It can be done through various ways, whether it be small group celebrations or large parties. Rewards and recognition are practiced differently for high-performing teams; they are more focused on team performance than on individual contributions. However, when it comes to high-performing teams, I am not asking you to discount individual contributions. There should be appropriate weightage given to individual performance, provided there is a significant contribution to the team's performance as well. This is where I see many organizations missing the trick. Be it social, business, political, or any other business—the reliance on individual behavior is given more importance than team performance. This is not the right way to build high-performing teams. When this happens, the performance of the team hinges on one person, and if that person leaves, the team's future is at risk.

I have a few case studies we can examine to understand these aforementioned points better.

CASE STUDY 1:

I was once working with a team that was undergoing major restructuring. It was within a global organization, and I was in charge of a team that was transitioning into a new organization. Once the transition was complete, I was left with a team wherein the members did not have a lot of technical skills. Basically, the members of my team were not wanted by the previous organization.

In other words, I was given the hand-me-downs. It was no surprise that the team I was in charge of did not have a positive attitude. They neither had the technical skills nor the fire in the belly to get the job done. So, I had to deal with the difficulties of transition as well as create a high-performing team. To complicate matters further, I was new to the job and was thus unaware of my team members' strengths and weaknesses.

Thus, the first thing I did was to assess the team. I found out where each member of the team stood, and I segmented them into three areas:

First, people who had the necessary skills for the job.

Second, people who did not have all the necessary skills but possessed the desire to excel. The third category included people who neither had skills nor the enthusiasm to excel. Then I faced the challenge of coming up with new roles. I identified that I needed people equipped with the right technical skills, and I also needed people who were passionate and who had been through a similar experience. We needed people who had the experience of handling a transition.

So, I had to outsource people and bring them on board soon. I also had to foster a healthy collaborative environment with the existing people by upgrading their skills parallelly. Those who could cope up and adapt to the new environment and those who were excited and filled with energy stayed with us. Those who did not eventually find a way out or were shown the way out. Within six to eight months, we were able to build a high-performing team, and this was reflected in the improved customer satisfaction score. When I took over, the customer satisfaction score was somewhere around two out of five. After six to eight months, the number rose to around 4 and almost 5. What did I do differently?

Well, first, I revisited the structure and put in place the right delivery model. Secondly, I did an internal SWOT analysis: Identifying Strengths, Weakness, and Opportunities and Finding Threats. This helped us find out which team members had the capabilities to take on new challenges. We found the people who had the potential and the attitude to fit in the team. Next, I looked into where I could invest in and develop such people.

Then I tackled the question of what to do with the people who did not fit in. I pondered on how the transition could be handled. If I were to offer an analogy, it would be like our bodies. We need to identify the cancerous cells in our body before they spread to other parts of the body. Similarly, we needed to cull cancerous units within the company. After taking all these steps, I finally focused on setting clear performance standards and goals for the team, which were aligned to the team members' individual performance. This gave the employees a sense of focus.

To help individuals identify themselves with the team, we undertook a lot of interventions and group brainstorming sessions. This helped align our objectives.

We set clear performance standards. Best performers were rewarded, and those who did not were asked for self-reflect and make a conscious effort to do better. No one was left alone. All the team members helped each other grow. I have always encouraged teamwork, and all the members of my team stood by each other. They focused on how all their joint efforts could better the team's performance. Although the team was not very large in terms of number, it was one of the strongest teams. Customer satisfaction went up over 100 percent. This way, a team that was staffed by the people who were on the lowest rung of the performance input was now a high-performing, winning team.

It was all about getting the basics right and developing resilience, and looking at things objectively, with honesty and fairness. Having said all that, it is also important to be humane and manage the team with empathy. To give an example, one of our team members, let's call him Jim, was going through a difficult time and was not able to focus on his work. I noticed this, and I asked Jim to take a sabbatical and deal with whatever he was going through. Although his position was vacant for a while, I did not hire a replacement. Other team members covered for Jim and took care of his work. After a few days, Jim returned to his job stress-free and resumed his duties.

I am sure his dedication to his work increased after this little incident. One cannot be a high-performer all the time. There may be some bad times. Because of momentary personal reasons, the performance levels of one of my top employees had dipped. I knew where he came from, so I let him have his space. Thanks to our group activities, the team was so strong that the other members stood by Jim and covered for him until he was ready to get back.

So, by employing the right techniques, I was able to create a high-performing team within 8 months. The team was self-reliable and empowered and could take on any task with no or minimal supervision.

CASE STUDY 2:

This is another case study about building high-performing leadership teams. One of my clients had a leadership team with 15% of leaders, all very capable and competent. However, they were all on the verge of retirement. They did not spend sufficient time in terms of building high-performing teams.

This put the organization's future at risk, as these capable leaders were set to retire in the next two or three years. Due to the lack of high-performing teams, the organization would have to hire leaders externally.

So, rather than waiting for the next two to three years, in certain cases, we identified would-be successors for critical roles externally. One of our key criteria while hiring successors was their capability to build strong teams under them. This was a skill set that was absent among the existing people. Either the skill was not there, or in certain cases, they wanted to hold on to a position for too long. Hiring successors was a good move because it gave us enough time to train them and prepare them to succeed the retiring leaders. Following this move, we had successors in place one year before the present leaders retired.

They were immediate deputies who could take over their role and simultaneously focus on developing a strong team under them. We actually saw performance levels increasing by 45%. This was not the case earlier. The senior leaders had kept everything to themselves, and they were holding on to information.

Once we implemented the new strategy, within one year, we saw a dramatic increase in performance because we hired leaders who at once spent time developing high-performing teams under them. This equipped them to create future successors for themselves. So, what did we do differently in terms of hiring? Well, instead of hiring people who were only capable of doing their current job, we looked at the potential. We made sure at least 1/3rd of the people we were hiring had bigger thoughts. We addressed the issue of creating capable successors for the future as well.

CASE STUDY 3:

I once worked with this large manufacturing organization, which was also a pioneer in the field. They had a strong market, a visionary leader, and clear strategies. They not only hired the best talents but also had certain well-established and innovative business and people practices. However, the reliance on the first-line leaders was very high, which gave rise to a few power centers within the organization.

As a result, there was no collaboration between the different business units; the consistency of performance varied from one unit to the other. It so happened that there was a recession, and one of the units was deeply affected.

Now, if that unit had been on good terms with the other business units, they would have received cover and help from them. However, that was not the case. Since there was no help received from anyone, that particular business unit incurred losses and eventually shut down. This resulted in 1000 people losing their jobs. This non-collaborative behavior gave rise to a lot of negativity within the organization.

As a result, in a few months, the organization lost its glory. It started losing its credibility and brand image in the market. It has been 25 years, and the organization still has not been able to bounce back. This case study shows us how important collaboration is within different business units.

CASE STUDY 4:

This case study is about a highly profitable startup; it was into data analytics with a company size of 150 employees. The organization's motto was to grow 10 times its top line and five times its bottom line in a span of three years. The organization was headed by a strategic and highly committed visionary leader. Unfortunately, the employees were not capable enough to scale the organization to the next level. They neither had the skill set nor the experience. If this organization had to realize its goals, they were in dire need of senior leaders, and it also had to create an additional layer of leaders within the organization who could manage the individual contributors and first-time managers.

However, the company did not want to let go of any people, so they continued investing in their existing employees. They also brought in a consulting team to help them build capabilities. After a careful assessment, we suggested that the CEO hire external resources. After several discussions, the CEO agreed to this proposal. Although this was an investment initially, the results were tremendous. This organization is on its way to reaching its goals today and also has a good global presence. They also made sure the current senior leaders were training their successors. This is the importance of having the right structure, strategy, experience, culture and capabilities.

CASE STUDY 5:

This is another case study on similar lines. There was another company of a similar size, which had a lot of home-grown talent. When it came down to globalization, the current leadership pool was not ready. The organization did not want to invest in hiring external leaders.

However, the current staff did not have the right capabilities. If I may quote Peter, "They had risen to the level of incompetence." They were good at practical roles and operational roles. But they were not good at strategic roles. They did not have the right executive personnel to deal with external stakeholders. Although they could be trained, this would have taken a lot of time. The organization eventually brought in a consultant. It was made clear by the consultants that the existing team was not up to the challenges.

However, the company did not take the advice. As a result, the organization could not achieve any of its strategic goals. The organization did not have the right leaders to help them handle the losses incurred, and neither could they handle the media.

This resulted in the organization losing credibility. So, what do we learn? The company should have hired external leaders at the right time. They should have assessed beforehand if their current employees could take on new roles. Being realistic and hiring at the right time while simultaneously training your internal team is important.

TAKEAWAYS:

- Ensure there are clear goals.
- Ensure there is the right team structure in place.
- Ensure one is able to create the right kind of culture of empowerment and the right kind of delegation of authority. Group consent is important, but this should not interfere with the speed of decision-making.
- Ensure that there is a conscious effort in developing teams, and whenever required, get external resources on board if your internal team does not have the capabilities.

3

OVERCOMING CHALLENGES IN CREATING HIGH PERFORMING TEAMS

"Show me someone who has done something worthwhile, and I'll show you someone who has overcome adversity."

- Lou Holtz.

In the previous chapter, we spoke about some of the common challenges we experience while forming high-performance teams. This chapter intends to highlight the different techniques or methods you could adopt to overcome those challenges. The first and foremost question that needs to be addressed is, **'how do we identify gaps in high-performing teams?'** Identifying gaps involves using various tools like psychometric instruments such as MBTI, Belbin, etc. Both these tools help identify the psychological makeup of the team members and help you understand the common gaps that exist within the different members. Some of the major areas often checked through this method include the team members' complementary strengths, missing links, and skills to overcome obstacles.

The MBTI or the Myers Briggs Type Indicator is a psychometric assessment tool that helps identify and measure individuals' psychological preferences.

Most importantly, it gives a clear idea of how people recognize the world and make decisions in their lives through their different assumptions.

Even though Catherine Cook Briggs and her daughter, Isabel Briggs Myers, are considered the creators of this test, it is based on the psychological theories of Carl Gustav Jung. In 1921, Jung published a book titled, *Psychological Types*, in which he mentioned the four principal psychological functions, namely, Sensation, Intuition, Feeling, and Thinking.

Jung's theory was hard to understand and difficult to apply in people's daily lives. Hence, the mother-daughter duo decided to make it simple so that every individual would realize its practical use. This decision led to the creation of the MBTI. As per records, this tool was first utilized during World War II. It was very useful for women entering the industrial workforce as the men were conscripted for the war. This tool enabled women to identify the most effective and comfortable war-time jobs they could take up for their livelihood.

The MBTI assessment helps analyze the individual's predominant psychological element in every four categories. They will be able to analyze whether their psychological self is an introvert or extrovert, sensory or intuitive, rational or imaginative, whether their thoughts or feelings rule their decisions, perceptive or judgemental, etc. All these aspects are analyzed, and a personality equation is formed. According to the MBTI assessment, there are sixteen types of personalities, and every individual will fall under any of these sixteen types.

Once the assessment is done, the managers will be able to understand the behavior of each member by knowing about their personality traits. When a manager can understand the employees' personalities properly, they will be able to communicate with the team members properly. As communication is the basis of good relations, it is a must to build good communication among the different members of the team. Understanding the personality of the team members also has another benefit. It enables the manager to have good knowledge about the skills of the members involved. This information will help in designating specific people who will complement the profile and responsibilities of the other. Such designations lead to an efficient, productive, and positive environment, which will benefit the team.

The MBTI also aids in identifying the stress behaviors of the team members and will also assist in increasing the Emotional Quotient of the members. One of the primary steps involved in creating productive teams is accepting the differences, either in the thinking process or the understanding process.

Once you accept this fact, the chances of establishing mutual respect will also increase. Mutual respect is a much-needed quality in every organizational set-up, as it opens up vistas for a more productive and harmonious environment.

Hence, individuals with different personalities are an added advantage for a team to be more efficient and effective.

Having an idea about a balanced and an imbalanced team might be useful when creating a high-performance team. Usually, some organizations tend to appoint analytical and rational people. Most of the companies in the technological field have this tendency.

However, even though they are analytical and logical, most are introverts. This kind of team is an imbalanced team, as they consist completely of thinkers and no feelers. What happens is that, in most cases, such people will only focus on facts and figures and hence will be in a hurry to make decisions quickly.

Even though they can validate the data provided by all the team members and move ahead with a unanimous decision, they often forget an important aspect of the decision-making procedure. They don't ponder how their decision could affect the rest of the employees and clients or how the targeted audience feels and responds to the formulated decision. That is why a feeler is also needed in the team with proper knowledge about the scope and role of feeling in the decision-making procedure. Hence, an imbalanced team always leaves a blind spot.

So, it is the duty of the manager or the group leader to accommodate feelers along with the thinkers so that "group thinking" can be avoided and an accurate decision can be taken. Another important tool useful for high-performance teams is the Belbin method.

This method is named after the famous management psychologist, Dr. Meredith Belbin, who in the early 1970s tried to discover a technique that could predict the successes of teams. For this purpose, he worked along with Henley Management College. A series of experiments was conducted to research where he used business simulations.

For the study, he divided the participants based on their psychological types, such as introverted, extroverted, etc. He aimed to find the perfect team with the ideal mix of psychological types. Within five years, he made an insightful discovery that specific patterns of behavior existed, which could be analyzed as a reason for the team success of some particular projects. He also understood that individuals tend to prefer one or more of these patterns that he discovered. He also commented that attaining perfection was a challenging process, and no single team could achieve that status for every task.

However, after much research, Belbin identified eight to nine clusters of behaviors that are needed for a successful team. He termed these clusters as team roles and defined them as "a tendency by an individual to behave, contribute or interrelate with others in a team in certain ways," according to the kinds of behavior attributed to certain job roles and based on how the particular role might manifest in a team.

Belbin's research reinforced the theory that the success of every team depended on the interdependence and mixed psychological types of the members.

He successfully predicted the success rates of the groups in the specific projects that were provided to them. Hence, after all the research, he asserted that the team members' individual strengths, when put together, could bring out wonderful results. If you want a high-performing team, you need first to check if your team is a balanced one or not.

Try to divide your team members according to the roles provided by Belbin.

You could do so based on the pointers given below:

- Identify the activities which you prefer to do and which you detest to do
- ask other team members about their concepts and feelings towards the different job roles
- Make sure that you can create a mixed team for a particular kind of task

As you are acquainted with the background of Belbin's model, let us now look at the meaning of each role and the preferences associated with them.

Belbin Team Roles: Summary

Thinking-oriented roles	Plant; Monitor Evaluator; Specialist
Action-oriented roles	Shaper; Implementer; Completer/Finisher
People-oriented roles	Coordinator; Team Worker; Resource Investigator

1. Thinking-Oriented Roles:

These are the innovators of every team. The team will only have steam if they are bubbling with new ideas. Hence, one of the primary roles of every establishment is to hire people for the thinking-oriented roles.

They will always ignite the spark of innovation and opportunity. Those who belong to this role are again classified into three- Plant, Monitor-Evaluator, and Specialist.

Plant: They are the source of innovations. Even though they are excellent at their work, most of them are introverts whose preference is to work alone. Amidst their introverted personality, they are interested in being highly acclaimed for their ideas and work. However, they will equally go down the dumps if they are criticized for their work. Some of the weaknesses of people who belong to this category are their inability to work within constraints, generating impractical ideas, etc.

Monitor Evaluator: This set of people is termed analyzers. They take up the responsibility of analyzing the innovative ideas generated by the plant group or others. They are the critics of the plant group, and they insist on checking the viability of the ideas that the plant group presents. Their weaknesses include a lack of drive, an inability to motivate others, and being overly critical.

Specialist: A group of thinking-oriented people armed with special skills in specialist jobs is called specialists. Their role is crucial because they possess special skill sets needed to fulfill their roles, unlike others. However, their role is vital only when a specialist is required, and their weaknesses include a lack of versatility and an inability to see the bigger picture.

2. **Action-Oriented Roles:**

They are the action heroes of every company. Unlike the thinking-oriented people, who come up with innovative ideas and work with their heads, these people are engaged in finishing the assigned projects. Instead of brainstorming, this group of people put their heads down and ensured that the project went well. The action-oriented role is divided into three types: shaper, implementer, and completer or finisher. Let us have a quick look at these three types.

Shaper: Being the challengers of the team, they perform well when they are under pressure. Unlike thinking-oriented people, the shapers of the action-oriented group are extroverts and are always interested in leading the group and cultivating the best outcome from the team. They are often questioning the existing norms and are also wise enough to be looking at challenges as opportunities.

Sometimes, they may come across as aggressive, but they only do so to make their dreams come true. However, it is good to have only a single shaper within the team, as an increased number of shapers will only result in constant arguments and no fruitful results. Being sharp and argumentative while being considered their strength can also be regarded as their weakness, as it might hurt the feelings of others.

Implementer: The action-oriented people who implement the ideas and plans of the shapers and thinking-oriented people are known as the implementers. Their primary role rests in converting the ideas generated by thinking-oriented people into actions. They are acknowledged for their systematic and well-organized manner of work.

If you want to attain your goals and hit your deadlines, assign your tasks to the implementers.

However, they are also notorious for being inflexible and resistant to change.

Completer/Finisher: They are the action-oriented people who ensure that the assigned projects are completed. In most cases, these people are detail-oriented and check all the tiny details before confirming that the project is completed. They are often nicknamed deadline-obsessed perfectionists, as they always pressure the team to get things done on time. They generally detest delegation as they prefer to do things on their own. Their weakness also includes the excessive unwanted worry they carry about the deadlines and the perfection of the project assigned to the group.

3. **People-Oriented Roles:**

They are the best communicators of every firm. People-oriented people roles are for those who enjoy working with others. They, too, can be categorized into three types: Coordinator, Team Worker, and Resource Investigator.

Coordinator: The role of coordinators is often considered to be a position that is in tune with that of team leaders. It is a position supported with respect afforded by the different team members. They are often approached when teams encounter any issues or obstacles. They are also acclaimed to be good listeners and are also good at recognizing the individual contributions of others. The primary responsibility includes coordinating and delegating the team's daily activities under the control of a more senior manager. However, sometimes they are found to be unloading their work in the guise of delegation.

Team Worker: You need this group within every organization to ensure the proper working of the firm. In most cases, they are noted for the personal sacrifices they make for the team's betterment. Being good listeners, they also help ease the issues between the team members and make sure that everything is working properly. Their weaknesses include being too diplomatic, and staying in an uncommitted position for a long period, hence being indecisive.

Therefore, it is always good to have a limited number of team workers in a team. The more the number of team workers, the lesser productivity of a team.

Resource Investigator: The main quality of a resource investigator is their ability to think outside the box.

Being extroverted, the resource investigator enjoys working with external stakeholders, thereby helping the team achieve their targets. However, they are notoriously known for being overly optimistic and for the unbalanced interest in the projects.

Hence, the real challenge lies in creating the "Ultimate Team."

CREATING THE ULTIMATE TEAM

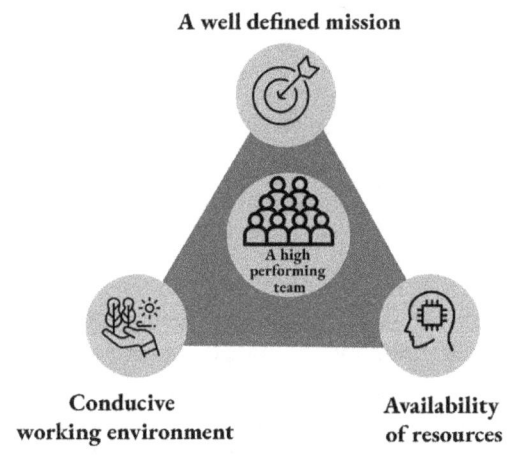

The definition and characteristics of the different job roles might have given you an idea about your team members, and now you must be in a position to put them in the category mentioned above roles. Belbin was far-sighted and predicted that people would prefer two roles- a primary and a back-up, rather than sticking on to one. Hence, you might feel that the same individual can be placed in one or more possible roles at the end of the day.

The question remains: How can we create the ideal team by combining these roles and placing the right candidate in the right role? It would be helpful to note Belbin himself was completely against the notion of an ideal team.

He claimed that certain factors should be reconsidered while combining a team for a specific project. Firstly, he asks the managers to connect people based on the nature and stage of the project.

For example, if the project involves a deadline, try to add more completers or finishers and shapers to complete the project within the time limit.

Likewise, if it is an innovative project or the firm is looking for creative ideas, try to add more thinking-oriented people and completers. He asserts that the manager should appoint coordinators or shapers to the leadership roles.

It would ensure a good rapport between the functional and team roles; it will enhance the communication between the different team members and ultimately lead to success. Belbin also suggests that each member should have a good idea about the rest's different roles and responsibilities. A proper understanding of one another will be beneficial, especially as they work together. Another technique that can be used for creating high-performing teams is 360° feedback. It is a widely used tool as it is a three-way feedback-manager's feedback on the team, team's feedback on the manager, and the input of the peer group of the team. A great positive impact of this tool is that it helps identify the gaps within the team.

Performance appraisal is another technique that aids in creating high-performing teams. Other techniques include focus group discussions and listening to the clients' feedback. So, in short, all these techniques help in identifying the gaps within a team. Once the gap is identified, the next task is to address them in high-performing teams. When a manager talks about gaps, it will create many doubts within the team members. Gaps could mean an absence of skills, problems with behavioral patterns, issues with attitudes, etc. Even though the gap mentioned here is associated with knowledge issues, the members might not identify what the manager conveys. One major reason for this is the team members' inability to assess their expectations. One of the primary issues associated with the lack of clarity is that the objectives are not laid out in stark detail.

In most cases, people consider that individual performance outweighs team performance. However, in reality, it is the reverse. As far as a person stays in a group, he should be thinking about the team performance, rather than individual performance. Hence, in situations where knowledge becomes the issue, proper training or feedback will address the problem. Coaching and mentoring will also be useful.

Apart from knowledge, skill can also become an issue. Identifying the gaps in the skill sets and addressing them will be a good way of approaching this issue. Team coaches could act as facilitators, provide proper training, and create a strong link between the different members of the team.

We often start the training process by enabling the members to understand what entails within their performance criteria.

We often portray the established result areas, where the individual results are linked with each other. Once they identify their result areas, we transfer the process to the next level, where the members get a clear idea of what type of behaviors are expected from them as team members. When addressing a skill gap, we offer proper training and mentoring sessions. However, the performance of the team members is thoroughly observed, and feedback is also provided promptly.

This feedback includes the aforementioned 360° performance reviews, customer feedback, employee satisfaction scores feedback, and the observed behavior within the team. In short, the gaps can be addressed in terms of knowledge and skills. However, while addressing them, make sure not to make personal comments to hurt the team members. Mentoring programs might not always be successful. Let me offer you five tips that you could adopt for implementing successful mentoring programs.

Recently, I read an article written by Lauren Trees, in which she references the adage "it takes two to tango" when speaking of mentoring programs. The concept that only two people are needed for dance is wrong, as the contributions of the music, the dance lessons, the endless practice, etc., are often neglected if we take the quote in its literal terms. Likewise, never think that mentoring programs only involve the participation of the mentor and the mentee. Without a strong basis of counseling, guidance, and support, no mentoring program will succeed.

So, the first tip that you could imbibe for implementing a successful mentoring program is to have a thorough understanding of the learning objectives. The mentor and the mentee should first agree upon the learning objectives they are targeting together. With a proper plan in mind, the duo could set clear goals and activities from day one onwards, and the outcomes received will often be outstanding. Having a clear target enables the mentoring pair to indulge in open discussions within a single frame of thought. Along with that, a clear learning objective helps mentors analyze the needs of the mentees and could further formulate and refine the mentoring process based on those needs.

However, if you have started the mentoring session without a proper learning objective, convert the next session into an open discussion platform where you both have to think and discuss the learning objectives. The mentoring pairs can begin their frank discussions only if they have a target in mind.

Learning objectives serve another purpose, too- it enables the mentors to confirm that they have ample knowledge about the learning objectives they are planning to get involved in.

The next tip for implementing a successful mentoring program is to set clear and rigid timelines. It is always advisable to have time-bound sessions rather than open-ended sessions. The timelines help in being aware of the urgency of deadlines and having a strong understanding of the progress milestones and results. However, this time-bound activity might extend from six months to one year in certain areas. A good example of this is the mentorship provided for career counseling. They are long-term mentorship programs as it is very important to create rapport and trust among the pairs.

The next tip is to make sure that the mentor and mentee are clear about the ground rules. Every organization should urge its mentors and mentees to have a clear notion about the ground rules needed for interaction. This will enable them to have a good idea about their roles and responsibilities as part of the mentoring program. Clear ground rules help them eliminate misunderstandings that might hinder the mentoring program's success.

The fourth tip that should be adopted is to provide sufficient training to the mentees and mentors. Both parties should be aware of their roles, expectations, mode of communication, relation-building tactics, etc. Without proper training, a mentor will not perform well, and the mentee will not learn anything.

Last but not least, the firm should provide adequate tools and resources for the mentoring program's success. These tools help support productive interactions and aid the mentor and the mentee through the different steps like interactions, goal tracking, progress, conversations, etc. I hope all these tips will be of great help to you when you think about implementing mentoring sessions in your organization.

I often encounter one important question: "Are mentoring and coaching the same?" If this question is asked to you, what will be your reply? If your answer is yes, then you are wrong. Often, we use the words 'mentoring' and 'coaching' interchangeably.

However, in reality, both are different as the working relationship is different in both cases. Even though concepts such as employee learning, career development, etc., are the same for both the processes, the focus role of the participants, approaches, and tools involved in both the methods are different.

For example, mentoring is an informal gathering which focuses on creating a mutually beneficial relationship that upholds long-term career achievements.

On the other hand, the International Coaching Federation defined coaching as "partnering with clients in a thought-provoking and creative process that inspires them to maximize their personal and professional potential. The process of coaching often unlocks previously untapped sources of imagination, productivity and leadership". Another major difference between the two is visible in the role of the participants who are part of the processes. In a mentoring session, the mentor will have prior knowledge about the needs of the mentee. Hence, emphasis will be given on active listening, making suggestions, creating connections, and offering information. However, in coaching, this prior knowledge will be absent. So, the coach has to follow other steps such as creating a rapport with the participant, identifying their needs by listening to them, and helping them create an action plan. Another difference is that, in coaching, the focus shifts from the coach to the client.

Mentoring often follows a self-directed modus operandi, in which the participants are equipped with the power of choices. However, in coaching, a structured process is followed, rather than the choice-driven option. In a mentoring program, the participants are asked to sign an agreement that lays down the rules and regulations that ought to be followed. The agreement also gives a clear picture of targeted goals, schedules of the meeting, learning content, and the method of communication. Whereas, in coaching, the agreement is laid down for setting rules for the partnership. Even though these components differ in mentoring and coaching, some comparable characteristics can also be found.

Target achievement is the final goal of both these processes, and hence, the defined roles enhance this achievement. In both methods, trust, open communication, and flexibility are needed. Both the processes require training, orientation, and education. So, in short, even amidst the differences, many factors connect mentoring with coaching, which ultimately aims to create high-performing teams. Apart from the skills and knowledge part, another gap is often found in the sphere of behavior. Behavioral issues are often addressed through counseling, mentoring, or coaching. A clear understanding of good behavior and contradictory behaviors is needed to strive in business and management.

A good way of pouring in the concepts associated with behavior is to share our own experiences and the assessments that we have conducted on pleasing behaviors, contradictory behaviors, positive behaviors, negative behaviors, etc.

Once the gaps are identified, the next task is to prioritize them in the high-performing teams. Prioritizing gaps in high-performing teams is all about immediately understanding what needs to be done to boost productivity and guide the team in the right direction. Prioritizing gaps also helps create the right culture and environment that enables team members to support one another and work together collaboratively. Many surveys have clearly stated that the correlation between the high-performing team members has resulted in increased customer satisfaction and business results.

I want to relate a case study concerning the efficiency of high-performing teams.

One of our clients, a leading organization in the tech industry with a legacy of over four decades of existence, experienced some gaps concerning their performance. The company has a workforce of more than 50000 had a highly capable leadership team comprised of highly qualified and experienced personnel. However, when the company identified gaps in performance, they sought my help to probe into the matter to understand the root cause. So, I started thinking about the different steps involved in creating a high-performing leadership team.

As a first step, I decided to study and identify the organization's organizational structure and business strategy. So, the primary questions that came into my mind were, "Is the business strategy challenging enough?", "Is the business strategy realistic?", "Were all the business leaders aligned to the common strategy of the organization?" etc. A study on the company's growth revealed that it was growing at a 10- 15% CAGR. In contrast, the market was growing at about 14% CAGR. We could conclude that the business was only gaining at a regular momentum. Hence, the first question I raised with the business leaders was, "Is your strategy a stretch strategy because the organization has been in business for a long time?"

They later realized that the strategy they were following was very conservative and that they only looked at growth at a transactional level. The second point that I realized was that the firm was focused more on driving bottom-line growth, comfortability, etc., which is, in a way, the right measure of success.

However, even with that focus, the business growth rate was not increasing at the desired pace.

So, I conducted an envisioning workshop, where the leadership team debated the organization's 3–5-year vision. This exercise helped the team in realizing their lack of stretch goals.

They also understood the gap and started thinking about the bigger picture. Then the leadership team started concentrating more on challenging the status quo and hunting for new markets to make their entry, the different marketing segments they needed to get into, the kind of products and services they would need, etc. So, when the existing strategy was questioned, a new strategy emerged, a three-year plan aimed at 100% growth. Challenging the current goals and strategies often paves the way for the right kind of stretch that ultimately leads to the right type of stimulus. Once the plan was ready, the leadership team started working on the details. They realized that it was a doable project.

However, the remaining questions were, "How do we establish capabilities for the newer offering?", "Should it be done through green filed expansion, or brown filed expansion?", "Should the plan concentrate more on building capabilities, completely from scratch?" These questions led to the conclusion that the organization needed to focus on generating funds and acquiring more companies.

Once the next step was assessed, a new business line emerged, which was predicted to have contributed about 30% of revenues from a zero base. Hence, for this purpose, the organization decided to provide the opportunity to redeploy some talents internally.

So, I hope you might be acquainted with the concept of "thinking differently" when it comes to strategies. Once the strategy was addressed, I moved to the organizational structure and target model. The key questions that needed to be addressed here were, "Is the current organization structure nimble?", "Is it agile?", "Is it empowering?", "Is it quick and decisive?", "Does it enable collaboration?" etc. When the leadership team started discussing these issues, they realized that the current structure was not enabling collaboration and their current working model functioned a limited amount of information sharing.

They kept their knowledge limited, and while many of them were delivering a good value to their individual client, it turned out that the two geographies were competing with each other rather than collaborating.

Consequently, the clients sometimes got confused. The organization created a matrix structure that encouraged decision-making while enabling collaboration and governance. This idea had a tremendous impact on the organization. Hence, it was understood that the organizational structure also needed a lot of reworking along with the new vision and strategy.

Another aspect that I looked into while dealing with this client was its work culture. Even though the performance was given great importance, much emphasis was laid on individual performance. Most performance-based incentives and promotions were based on individual performance rather than group performance. So, with inputs from the organization, we increased the weightage of organizational performance for the leadership team and team performance on the individual or functional teams. Thus, rather than just focusing on key performance indicators, the components of collaboration were added as a strong behavioral measure for the growth of an individual and a deciding factor for promotions.

Once the work culture expanded, the next step was to reconsider the technological and production processes. For this, an innovation cell was created to look at newer business opportunities. A strong business excellence team was designed to look at process improvements in the existing line of business. A strategy cell was also formulated to identify Merger and Acquisition opportunities by closely looking at corporate finance, corporate people, human resource functions, and operations. All these three newly formed teams helped the organization achieve its business goals. Interestingly, the organization registered a 35% CAGR growth during the pandemic and currently strives to achieve its business goals.

So, in short, the right strategy, structure, and culture of collaborative performance are the key contributors to every organization's success. So many other examples can be drawn from the real-life experiences of people and companies around us.

One among them is Jack Welch. In his famous book *Winning*, he talks about having a voice and dignity. As an employee, the individual should ensure that his voice is being heard and respected for all his efforts. Welch claims that companies that constrain voices from being listened to are not working in the proper direction. Along with that, he also offers a note for leaders. He mentions that being a leader means being deemed more responsible, where your primary duty is to think about others more than yourself.

Many maestros have provided much such leadership and organizational tips in this genre. I would also like to point out the example set by Hindustan Uniliver Ltd., the company widely appreciated for constantly improving their status and products in the business world. They are also known for introducing new products and their organized system of internally grooming talent. Hence, all the senior management roles are mostly filled internally. They are also acclaimed for the structured program they offer for developing leaders, including cross-functional training, technical training, functional training, international assignments, etc. Hence, all those aligned with the organization get the right experience, the right kind of training, and the right kind of coaching and mentoring support in their journey towards leadership. So, most of the CEOs of several organizations are found to have a Unilever background. In fact, an organization's ability to create high-performing teams and leaders is also a measure of success.

Another example that is oft-quoted with high performance is that of ICICI bank. As one of the largest private-sector banks, it includes a scientific process of grooming leaders and creating high-performing teams. Unlike other private banks, the staff are given stretched goals, stretched targets, and ample opportunities to succeed. The organization is widely praised for the calculated risks that they take in grooming leaders. Opportunities are often provided to internal candidates rather than external ones. So ICICI's leaders are home-grown and have grown internally within the organization.

TAKEAWAYS:

- I hope you are now thorough with the concepts such as identifying gaps over knowledge, skill, or attitude; the significance of setting clear performance goals, which are focused not only on individual performance but also on team performance, right behavioral indicators, contradictory behavioral indicators, etc.
- Make sure that your organization's reward system is based on merit and high performance, and ensure to offer career paths for high-performing teams and high-performing leaders. Let those success stories be shared among the other members of the organization to inspire them to be leaders in the future.
- Ensure that you have the right strategy to support high performance and a set stretch strategy because having an incremental plan will not drive high performance.

Sometimes you might have to go beyond your market growth rate, like the case study I have shared with you.

- Ensure that your organizational structure is right, enabling high-performing teams to succeed by making the right decisions.
- Also, be cautious about the work culture practiced in your organization, and remember that only a collaborative culture will bear the desired fruits. Then you should ensure that you have the right kind of mechanism, one which will lead you to your rewards, career paths, and ultimately success.
- Last but not least, continue your focus on developing the different teams through job rotations, training, executive coaching, mentoring, etc. These steps should be taken sustainably, and a regular and periodic check is needed to achieve success.

4

DEFINING HIGH PERFORMANCE IN TEAMS AND SETTING PERFORMANCE STANDARDS AND GOALS

"Alone we can do so little, together we can do so much."
— Helen Keller

I want you to consider a sports team, say a football team. Typically, you have specialized players assigned to play in specific positions like the midfield or carry out particular functions like attack or defense. Some of their duties might overlap.

However, any high-performing football team will have specific roles for each player on the team. They will have a set pattern and position they assume based on the ball's position on the field. They are expected to carry out their duties as part of their role, which is part of the larger game strategy. The strategy could be to defend, counter-attack, or attack. In a successful, high-performing team, members will be pretty clear about their goals, regardless of the scenario.

While a team might be playing in a tournament with their end goal being winning the trophy, they will not let themselves be distracted by it as they would be focussing on their immediate or short-term goals. Within this example of a tournament, it could be winning the next match. They know the long-term goal; still, they plan for short-term accomplishments, which ultimately contribute to their larger goal.

From this analogy, it is important to understand that setting the right goals and performance standards is important for a high-performing team.

In most scenarios, performance is considered completion of a certain task as efficiently as possible. This feat is acceptable on most days in most teams. However, having average or mediocre goals is insufficient for a high-performing team. For a high-performing team, crossing the finish line is the bare minimum. High-performing teams are about how exceptionally they cross the finish line and go further beyond. While race is an effective analogy for life, reality will surprise you with more than one finish line to cross.

If you remain stagnant in such a world, you will be left behind. So, while having achievable goals is realistic and a good boost to your self-worth and motivation, it is almost useless for a high-performing team not to dream big, involve risks, and chase the stars. If you conveniently set achievable goals, you are not challenging yourself, and there is only so far you can go without a challenge.

When I say challenge yourself, I do not mean you must set unrealistic goals. Challenging yourself can include performing tasks that you previously avoided because you either feared them or were lethargic. We often fall behind because we are afraid of the results or are too lazy to try out something new. When we talk about goals, we refer to SMART goals—Specific, Measurable, Attainable with a stretch factor, Result-oriented, and Time-bound.

In setting performance standards, one needs to figure out their stretched goals. We often see two types of people in a team: the members who just do their part and those who improve their skills and go the extra mile beyond what was assigned. An important characteristic that I have observed in high-performing teams is that they go beyond conventional teams by setting challenging goals and standards. Let us consider another sports analogy.

If you are looking at winning a 100-meter sprint, try to benchmark yourself against the best in class. What is the current world record, and how can you better the current world record? Benchmark yourself against the best.

Set high standards which require a lot of effort, hard work, perseverance, and the right kind of a stretch. Set specific criteria and metrics that will help you define what success looks like and start working toward it by setting short-term goals.

When you intend to outdo your goals, you beat yourself, and, in turn, your team will benefit and reciprocate. High-performing teams are very clear about what success is and how they will measure it. They are not easily distracted from the big picture. That is why these teams are not easily satisfied with readily achievable goals. High-performing teams keep looking at how to better their last performance, either in productivity, efficiency, or improvement in their skills. In a way, they compete with themselves and break their own record each time. This healthy practice ensures that these teams show continuous growth.

In a recent conversation with a high-performing individual and high-performing team, I was informed that one of the team goals was to question themselves at every step. It was not to say that they doubled back and doubted themselves, no.

Instead, some of the questions they asked themselves about their performance standards were, "How will I become more qualified at my current job?" "Have I acquired at least one new skill that might help me become better?" "How good am I compared to the best in class, globally?" As we can see, these questions allow space for introspection, improvement, and even individual growth as you answer these questions with action. High-performing teams are highly focused on staying relevant to the times and to their goals.

They do not try to do too many things. They prioritize and look at making an effort in the right direction. There is no point in spending extra effort in areas that will not give them the desired results.

Another thing about them is all their goals are time-bound. They always keep themselves on track and also set themselves a challenging timeline. The essence of handling deadlines can be seen here. These are all the relevant measures of success in setting high-performance goals for the organization. Keeping track of your progress is crucial when following the relevant measures that will eventually lead to your success.

However, it can be a tricky business. If not done properly, you will most likely lose important data and lose sight of your goals. There are various methods through which you may be able to follow up on your progress.

These are the Balance Scorecard, Objectives and Key Results (OKR), and Metamorphosis Performance Potential Framework.

Let us explore these methodologies.

BALANCE SCORECARD:

It is one of the frameworks that is used to keep track of strategic goals. These goals are measured and modified accordingly as the organization progresses. This framework allows the organization to stay in touch with its financial strategies, customer service, and product analysis. There are four different perspectives, and the names can vary according to what fits the organization's culture. In typical terms, the four perspectives are financial, customer, business process, and learning and growth.

While the financial perspective is about how the organization appeals to the shareholders, customer analysis is how the organization achieves customer satisfaction.

The business process consists of various processes necessary to improve and exceed customer retention and service and financial requirements. Learning and growth allow improvement in terms of employee training, technology, and infrastructure.

OBJECTIVES AND KEY RESULTS (OKR):

As the name suggests, this framework is divided into two parts, Objectives and Key Results. The objectives are a set of goals you want to achieve at the end of a defined period; typically, they are set monthly or quarterly. The key results are ways you can accomplish those goals. It is necessary to set your key results to be quantifiable and realistic. But do not hesitate to make it challenging at the same time. Risks can bring out unexpected great outcomes if you plot them wisely. Every objective must contain a set of key results and an indicator that can tell you the progress's whereabouts. The indicator can be updated as you climb up the ladder. Remember that these objectives and key results are not set in stone and can change when necessary. OKR is one of the most popular frameworks because of its simplicity, the transparency it provides to the employees, and the fact that it can be used as a performance review.

It is used by companies like Google, LinkedIn, and Twitter.

PERFORMANCE POTENTIAL FRAMEWORK:

We use this framework. We call it linking the strategy, structure, culture, technology, and processes required to drive peak performance and maximize potential in teams.

9 BOX GRID

Potential \ Performance	Low	Moderate	High
High	"Potential Gem" — High potential / Low performance	"High Potential" — High potential / Moderate performance	"star" — High potential / High performance
Moderate	"Inconsistent Player" — Moderate potential / High performance	"Core Player" — Moderate potential / Moderate performance	"High Performer" — Moderate potential / High performance
Low	"Potential Gem" — High potential / High performance	"Potential Gem" — Low potential / Moderate performance	"Potential Gem" — Low potential / High performance

(9-BOX GRID discussed in detail in chapter 10)

In this framework, there are some key questions that we ask high-performing teams:

- Do you have the right strategy in place to achieve the attainable result and time-bound goals?
- Do you have the right organizational structure and target-operated model to deliver what you need to do?
- Do you have the right kind of culture? Do you operate on a culture that rewards teamwork and collaboration, and which rewards team performance, and the culture which challenges the status quo?
- Do you have the right kind of processes and the right kind of technology to enable success?

We then discuss these four areas in the context of high-performing teams and give them the time and space to contemplate. Once the team has come up with answers to these questions, they will navigate their way by setting up relevant measures to lead to growth.

The next area we focus on is potential: It is the capability to perform well at the current job and do well at the next level. Many people are not aware of their full potential for a long time in their lives. Many spend their entire lives without unlocking their true potential.

To avoid such a scenario and to live a successful life, you must constantly challenge yourself and allow yourself to step out of your comfort zones. It could be as simple as exploring different fields that you did not have the chance to before. No matter how bizarre it seems, give it a shot. You might surprise yourself with a hidden talent. By working on your good and bad habits, you will thrive in critical areas and release your true potential, which will help you in the present and the long term. These are the important ingredients needed to measure success in individuals and teams.

When all these ingredients get together, one can build a high-performing team and set challenging, stretched goals.

CAREER PROGRESSION FRAMEWORK:

Step 1: When we talk about building a team, it is about setting the right kind of performance measures and goals, defining what these goals look like, and defining and engaging the way of working with each other. It is crucial to set the right performance measures to move the team toward triumphantly achieving its goals.

We have discussed some methods to trace the performance of your team. It is necessary to choose the right measure that works for you amongst the available techniques. You can either rely on research and find what feels relevant to your organization or find a plan that suits you the best by trial and error. Every organization has something unique to offer, which is why your goals will also be singular.

The easiest way to plot your goals is to imagine your future: where do you want to see yourself and your team in a few months/years? That could be your starting line to form a set of goals that align with your vision.

It is important to define what they look like and how you want to pursue them.

Step 2: Define how agreements and disagreements are resolved and how conflicts are resolved. The answer to resolving conflicts lies in communication. Being clear about your expectations and setbacks is the easiest way to avoid a conflict in the first place.

However, it is important to understand how conflicts arise. Conflicts in the workplace can be of two types, substantive and emotional. Substantive conflicts may arise over disagreements related to work. In a team, you will find a set of people who are more aggressive about risks than the others are. Everyone has a different approach to a problem, but you must land on one that benefits the team. Emotional conflicts may emerge from a place of insecurity, jealousy, or mental exhaustion in a person.

The best way to resolve disputes would be to communicate with the other person. Communication does not mean just expressing your views; it also means listening to what the other person wants to convey. A team must be a safe space for employees to express their opinions. It is essential to practice responding instead of reacting. It becomes important to take a step back and remember the big picture in a conflict.

Step 3: Get the teams to perform regular jobs. Remember the sports team analogy. Every team member plays a significant role. It is important that one sticks to that role and prioritize fulfilling it above everything else. Yes, by all means, you may hope to exceed the expectations and challenge yourself with more. But this should only come after you have completed your primary task. Teamwork does not just end there. Giving feedback to one another catalyzes the team's progress. It does not allow for too many mistakes but permits plenty of freedom for collaborative efforts.

For a team's exponential growth, its members must help one another when any one of them gets stuck. They need to leverage one another's strengths and help one another in their areas by providing continuous feedback and the right kind of encouragement and support. It also builds bonds within a team. Such bonds would enable a team to navigate the absence of a member or obstacles with minimum fuss.

Step 4: Benchmark your performance constantly and look to improve continuously. As we have discussed, in the case of a high-performing team, you are mostly set to break your own record. However, you will inevitably find a lot of competitors catching up with your achievements.

Competition has been trendy for a whole decade, and it does not look like it will lie low anytime soon. It is important to constantly benchmark yourself against your competitors and take every restorative measure to overtake them in such a competitive world. Benchmarking work is very different from comparing.

Comparing yourself with others might come from a place of insecurity or jealousy. However, benchmarking yourself against others is a way of owing to do better and improving yourself. As a team, defend the changes and also adapt to the newer trends. This process will help you stay relevant. When you start looking at benchmarking as a challenge, you will see the thrill of overcoming it and the endless learning possibilities you will have along the way.

DEFINING A SENSE OF PURPOSE IN THE TEAM

I have seen that teams without a purpose or a goal will never achieve success or high standards. If they achieve their goals, it will be more by accident than design—something that is not sustainable in the longer run. In Chapter 1, we discussed the story of the moon landing. Another popular story has been retold many times about when President Kennedy visited NASA.

He encountered a man with a broom and a bucket in a hallway and stopped to have a conversation. When asked what he did at NASA, the janitor humbly replied, "Sir, I helped put a man on the moon." You see, even though the role of a janitor is perceived to be small from societal standards, no role is ever really small. Your contribution is never insignificant.

The janitor had an understanding of the big picture. He understood that even if he was not qualified to contribute to the mission directly, his work still mattered and added up to the success. A team must develop such an understanding.

In a team, our roles and responsibilities may vary. But we must develop an intent toward our team. The only way you will contribute to the best of your abilities is by developing a sense of purpose in your workplace. A sense of purpose in the team is not only about achieving goals that are standard and conventional. It is not only working purely for a reward or recognition. Having a sense of purpose also involves being clear about the work plan and knowing why you are doing certain things.

All companies have their beginnings in a dream. While companies have partial responsibility to pass that dream down to their employees with enough trust, the duty also falls on the employee to remember why they wanted to be there in the first place and where they are headed.

When teams find a sense of purpose, they will find a way of achieving those goals. Goals become transactional without purpose. If teams adopt shortcut approaches, they will never be able to reach their full potential. Individuals may be successful but not the entire team.

CASE STUDY:

A mid-size organization worked mainly on payroll packages and analytics, catering largely to the corporate sector. This organization was full of highly capable people.

One could feel their high spirit through their products, sales strategy, customer service teams, and enabling functions (finance, technology, and human resources). So, with these teams here, teams that look like they were made to order, I think a critical factor which one is looking at is, how do they enable success?

They were doing well for a financially profitable organization, going back to 10%-15%. A lot of their business came in through references, so they were growing at the market growth rate—nothing wrong with that.

However, they sought my help to train the CEO to increase the turnover by 3 to 5 times in the next five years. We started the conversation and began analyzing the organization. We got deeper in terms of understanding their business strategy, the delivery model, benchmarks in the industry, the potential of the market, current customer base, customer retention ratios, the financial ratios of the organization, and more. After spending a good amount of time understanding these factors, we identified one of the key reasons they could not deliver to their full potential while doing reasonably well financially. They did not set stretched goals. The business was going on by itself.

The teams were doing well in managing the business, which was reflected in their customer retention ratios. The client retention ratio was 95%. So, what steps should they take to reach a growth of 3X to 5X? I thought the problem lay in how they attracted clients. Their three-decade-long existence was the key mode through which they were generating clients. It had grown largely on account of the credibility they could develop during this period. There was no doubt that they had exceptionally good customer service.

But their excessive reliance on getting customers only through references was not helping them grow exponentially. So, the first thing we did was to organize a visioning workshop for the team. It was all about getting the team to think and envision differently.

We wanted the members to step out of the box. We made sure not to use a single PowerPoint slide during this workshop. We wanted to ditch the conventional methods of presentation. We used white charts, and we used flip charts. We used a whiteboard. The task was simple. They were asked to draw up a vision for the organization. They had to draw it literally. It resulted in some interesting sketches. While we could spot some hidden talents and potential Picassos in the making, the drawings were hilarious in some other cases. But this exercise was not for testing their sketching ability. We were focused on their ability to put down their vision on paper. And exercise resulted in an unexpected turn of events. Earlier in our conversation with the CEO, we had talked about a 3X to 5X growth vision for the organization. However, this task helped them create an inspiring vision, and the team came out with a 10X vision for growing the business in the next 3-5 years.

It was a wonderful start; we kept challenging this vision. We did a SWOT analysis to determine the strengths of the organization. What were some of the weaknesses in the organization? What are the external opportunities that are available to them?

And what are some of the market threats which could possibly come? It is safe to say that the SWOT analysis paved the way for everyone to believe and find faith in what seemed an extremely challenging vision. The process to grow exponentially had started. The third thing that we focused on was understanding the process and the steps to make the vision a reality. It involved loads of brainstorming sessions. We divided them into smaller teams, including cross-functional teams. We laid out a detailed roadmap in a two-day workshop. It was a short amount of time and very intensive; the workshop was only about 12 hours long, with dinner and drinks thrown in.

But at the end of the workshop, we had managed to create a clear roadmap that provided a clear vision. It also included what kind of products were needed. What are the newer segments to focus on? What should be their market? Certain segments like the government sector and some small and medium-sized enterprises that might possibly want to avail their products and services were left untapped. Also, neighboring markets in Asia, which could leverage their products and services, were left untapped.

A new team was created to look at new business opportunities and new business initiatives. There was a change in the strategy of the organization. It was no longer functioning only on client reference, but it was ready to take off beyond the existing traditional multinational clients and large corporates.

We were moving into other verticals, like the government sector and small and medium enterprises, and looking at markets outside India. The focus was on markets like Bangladesh, Nepal, Sri Lanka, and, to a smaller extent, Bhutan and countries like Vietnam and Malaysia, where there was a good scope for the products offered by this organization. With this in mind, a detailed version of the roadmap was created. Cutting to the final result, in three years, the company grew 6X and was well on track to achieve its goal of 10X in five years. And that is despite the impact of Covid-19. Interestingly, the productivity also improved because one was doing more work with fewer people. The Covid pandemic did not impact this organization, which now continues to grow profitably even during this time.

A FEW KEY TAKEAWAYS FROM THIS CASE STUDY:

I will talk about other details of the case study here. The key result areas were clearly defined during the two-day workshop and beyond.

The model shifted from looking at individual performance to team performance by establishing interdependence upon each other. The focus was on the key result areas or key performance indicators and the behavior one must consistently demonstrate to achieve those goals. Areas like collaboration, trust, challenging each other, and innovation were all given importance in getting close to these goals. There was a clear framework for rewards and recognition, both financially and non-financially. Financial rewards included performance-based annual bonuses and stock options of the organization.

Non-financial rewards consisted of instant recognition rewards, awards that people could celebrate with their families. They were also presented with the opportunity to attend any event of their choice, like important matches or a musical concert that they found interesting. We see here that the value of the award was pre-determined. But they were also offered the choice of attending it with their families so that they could have a reason to celebrate with them. It added so much more value to it. In addition, a letter and a bouquet were delivered to their house so that there was a personal touch.

It went a long way toward building a strong level of commitment and developing appropriate behaviors that we had identified as essential contributors to their success. The other part of this journey that cannot be left out is the mistakes made. Management did not punish their mistakes. There were no consequences. Nobody got fired in the organization for making mistakes. It was not like anything was allowed, and errors were given a blind eye. They did not tolerate negligence and indiscipline. The expansion in strategy also meant that the teams had to hire people from outside. A few experienced people were employed.

Teams were focused on the development of the others by providing their input. People were given the freedom and flexibility; however, they performed under the watchful eyes of the manager. The organization took the necessary steps to help people attend the right kind of courses that were self-identified or identified by the HR department. Coaches and mentors were appointed.

Team members held each other to account, and they were there to support each other, rather than harshly criticizing each other and falling into the loop of the blame game. Anyone not abiding by this was called out and the expectations set were very clearly reminded to them. If someone were not measuring up, the rest of the team would be putting in the extra effort to help that person rather than finding fault. This drove a very positive culture within the organization.

TAKEAWAYS:

- First, set a visionary or inspiring goal. Anything that is going to be easily achieved will not be inspiring or innovative. Add a bit of risk. Step out of your conventional methods. The advantage of setting such a goal is that it helps you unleash your full potential. Remember, high-performing teams keep revisiting their goals.
  They are not satisfied with the status quo.
- Secondly, create goals that align well with all the team members. It helps you avoid conflicts. Aligned goals also do not operate independently. Aligned goals have the right people working on the right things. It is a system that can ensure ideal contribution from each of the team members.
- The third point is that a high-performing team carries an equal weightage for team performance and individual performance.

While individual performance alone cannot guarantee your growth, how significantly you have brought a change to your team and the organization matters the most.

- Fourth, the rewards and consequences are defined very clearly.
  This keeps the team motivated and also makes them feel appreciated. Appreciation goes a long way. It is a form of respect and expression of trust.
- The fifth point is to ensure the right kind of culture, collaboration, and trust within teams. Teams must support one another rather than be in conflict or point fingers.
  Conflicts are inevitable, but they are also resolvable. It all depends on how you resolve it. Managers and leaders play a very important role in facilitating the right kind of culture, collaboration, and trust.
- Teams must celebrate success. It is about celebrating success not just financially but also through non-financial rewards.
  As mentioned before, getting the family involved in celebrating success can add great value in expressing your commitment to your employee.
- High-performing teams learn from their mistakes. They learn from both positive experiences and from the calculated errors or mistakes they have made.
- Calculated risks are important as they enable you to stretch that extra mile. Every successful business is built from learning from mistakes and not from committing errors. Your failure is not your downfall but an opportunity to rise even higher.
- We see how high-performing teams do not get punished for their failures but are also not soft in areas of negligence or ill-discipline. Another area of high-performing teams is balancing youth and experience and ensuring an alignment of skill and cultural diversity. So, one needs both skill diversity and cultural diversity.
  One needs to go beyond the standard stereotype of diversity.
- A key enabler of diversity is getting multi-skilled and multicultural resources, which can help you think differently to drive high-performing teams.
- It is also important to follow a culture of meritocracy where people are hired, promoted, rewarded, and encouraged for merit rather than likes, dislikes, and conscious and unconscious biases.

- Conscious efforts have to be taken in the organization where managers and team members play the role of conscience gatekeepers. When the culture of meritocracy gets compromised, the most skilled resources will not achieve the best possible or desired goals.
- High-performing teams focus on strengths rather than dwelling only on weaknesses. And that is the importance of having people with different skills.
- If one member is strong in one particular skill and another member is not as skilled, they will complement each other. Rather than focusing on their weakness, they will focus on getting another strong individual in the same area.

  When a person can play to their strengths, they can get results far more quickly. That is the advantage of teams when compared to individuals. When teams are fitted to have complementary strengths, it will without a doubt drive exponential performance.
- Team members hold each other accountable in setting and delivering high standards while actively practicing interpersonal development and supporting each other.

  If something is not working out, it is called out in advance, and the required measures are taken. In an ideal scenario, the team members report any sort of bad news early to give everybody the right amount of time to address those concerns.

  And a person can handle those concerns proactively rather than reactively.
- Last but not least, the role of leadership is most important. Leadership works in co-creating an inspired vision. It is also about communicating it effectively, setting the right performance standards, coaching, developing, and motivating the team. Leadership also involves handling conflicts constructively and positively while providing a safe environment where people can collaborate, trust, and challenge one another on the status quo. Leaders also foster an environment where both the team and the individual are rewarded for their high performance through financial rewards and non-financial rewards.

PART B:
DEVELOPING HIGH PERFORMANCE TEAMS

5

ATTRACTING TALENT AND RECRUITING A HIGH-PERFORMING TEAM

Mission success is all about three main things:
- *Hiring people with diverse and complementary skills.*
- *Providing them with the right platform to unleash their potential.*
- *Helping them with the right opportunities and enabling them to taste success.*

- Ajay Bakshi

We have seen the characteristics of a high-performing team and understood what really brings out their essence. That is not the tough part. The tough part is to form a high-performing team. Attracting talent and hiring for the right profile are key ingredients in building high-performance teams. The team members are vehicles that will drive the team forward. Often, this criterion is rather neglected, and one spends a disproportionate amount of time and effort developing talent or managing underperformance. In the speed and urgency to hire people, one ends up hiring candidates who neither have the skills nor the right attitude toward the job.

Such hires are often a result of bad judgments made during the hiring process due to the pressure of desperate requirements, and consequently, this becomes a very expensive proposition.

The key differentiator for success is irrespective of the level (leadership, mid-management, and entry), hiring the right people, and having the best possible team working for you. It can contribute to the team from a financial perspective and save a lot of time. As a result, you can enhance your customer experience, which will directly contribute to your growth. An organization's success is built on several pillars: right strategy, right product, right processes, the right technology, right customers, etc. But talent is the key differentiator. It brings out the unique factor of an organization that helps them stand out from everyone else. All the other aspects may be replicated easily. But replicating talent is not easy. Talent gives a person a differentiating edge, so it is important to take your time to find it. Of course, a fair bit of things can be outsourced. Even knowledge can be outsourced and acquired. But a high-performing team cannot be outsourced. It needs the right set of minds to create one. Therefore, attracting talent and ensuring that the right people join your team is more than half the battle won.

Let us understand in-depth why it is important to hire talent. And, what should one be looking for?

Invariably, we look at experience. We look at technical skills, we look at functional skills, and we have a look at industry experience. Most of our interviews and discussions largely focus on "do they have the right experience and qualifications and have they done this in the past?" While these are critical areas to dissect, judging a candidate's flair might be insufficient. Often, we tend to ignore areas like culture fit, learning orientation, the ability to learn and unlearn, and simply, the potential of an individual. There is a reason why these areas may help you better evaluate a candidate than the former criteria mentioned.

Let us understand why.

Cultural fit enables you to determine how well the person will fit into the team. Basically, you are conducting a thorough inquiry into what languages the person can communicate in and how good they are at communicating a point across without causing conflict.

What formality and informality are they used to, and will they be able to mold themselves according to your organizational needs?

Do their expectations align with the organization's objectives? What is their definition of success and reward? How do they prioritize and schedule? How organized are they? These are some of the aspects that need to be considered before hiring a candidate. It gives a peek into what sort of person they are and how well they can blend into the team without losing their individuality.

Similarly, learning orientation demonstrates a person's thirst to learn and, more importantly, their ability to build on as they go forward. Curiosity to learn is what permits growth. But while learning is important, unlearning the bad conditioning and habits is also vitally important and comparatively harder. The willingness to unlearn unnecessary habits says a lot about the person on a higher level, and hence it becomes a plus point. All of these factors can be the basis for determining the strength or potential of the candidate. But what does potential exactly mean? It is important to understand that many roles do not necessarily require experience or an advanced degree. In fact, having experience does not directly translate to having potential.

Employees with extensive experience have often underperformed or performed at a mediocre level during their tenure. Thus, it becomes important to look at the quality of performance rather than the period of their experience. We should be hiring a person capable of doing the current job, but rarely do we assess this potential in an interview. Performance must be measured from a perspective of growth. Do they have the capability to progress to one or two levels above the prospective job? Do they sound like they would be open to leadership roles in the future? Will they dedicate themselves to your organization for the long term?

It may not be possible to hire everyone with high potential; sometimes, it is impossible to accurately determine a person's potential. But at least one-third of the team you are hiring should have a high potential. They must be marching toward the goal and have the full capacity to do bigger and broader jobs in the future. This will minimize the need to hire outsiders when there are vacancies. As a plus, you will be able to develop a very strong team internally.As mentioned, hiring is a key differentiator when it comes to creating high-performing teams. It is easy to get sidetracked and commit a mistake during the hiring process.

So, what must we do to ensure all the measures are in place to carry out the recruitment? Simple, we consult the tools.

One can use multiple tools and methods. A lot of them are based on judgment. To avoid bad judgments, organizations have several rounds of interviews with different stakeholders at different times. They also use business simulations, case studies, and leverage role plays. At the entry level, organizations also look at group discussions as enablers or eliminators and cognitive ability tests to assess skills like problem-solving, decision-making, etc.

I have seen that these tools help make interview processes seamless, efficient, smooth, and quick, and one is likely to attract the best talent. I emphasize attracting the best talent because interviews must end on a mutual good note. The candidate and the organization must feel equally engaged with each other. I have known organizations that have many rounds, say 12-15 rounds of interviews. By the time good candidates reach the sixth or the seventh round, the disengagement begins. Candidates tend to get restless and sometimes even give up hope.

At these times, those actively seeking job opportunities tend to take up other jobs in organizations that have been quicker to reach back to them. This is why it is crucial to adopt tools that are way more efficient than the current methods. Let us explore these tools in detail.

1. Psychometric or personality tests:

These tests consist of several rounds, including personality tests, critical thinking, and decision making. The organization has the flexibility to create a test based on what they are trying to understand about the candidates; thus, the test pattern is not set in stone. There are several good psychometric and personality tests available in the market. I have mentioned a few earlier, but in addition to these, there are many more that may be more suitable for your hiring model. These personality tests help you identify leadership behaviors, leadership derailers, motives, values, and preferences of individuals. This will also help you identify if they are a good cultural fit within the organization and if they are motivated enough to undertake the role. These are vital factors that you have to understand about the candidates. I have noticed that psychometrics does have a good advantage because you get data points that conventional interviews do not pick up. Some of them can get revalidated in a competency-based interview or a behavior-based interview.

So, I have found psychometrics can play a significant role in successfully identifying and hiring high-potential candidates.

2. Cognitive ability tests:

Cognitive tests are useful as they help you determine the candidate's logical thinking ability, problem-solving capability, analytical skills, and numerical aptitude. These are very necessary and indispensable attributes, especially in technical job roles. These sorts of tests help determine a person's general mental ability in mathematical computations, verbal compositions, and reading comprehension. Often, cognitive ability tests are taken by a group of people together and may act as an elimination round. The questions are set and scored based on the company's requirements.

The individual will be judged and asked to proceed if they pass this test.

3. Competency-based interviews:

These interviews test for the specific competencies required for the job role. Every organization has its own set of competencies: knowledge, skills, behavior, and attributes necessary to succeed in the organization. Usually, positive behavioral indicators and negative behavioral indicators help understand how a candidate fits into the role. Behavioral indicators check if the candidates demonstrate the required qualities. The competencies could include strategic thinking, the ability to manage and adapt to change, the ability to deal with ambiguity, the ability to lead teams, etc. All these aspects can be picked up in these interviews. The other way is the conventional interview. The candidate's previous achievements or experiences are tested through a series of questions to understand how they approached shortcomings and successes in the past. The focus is on technical expertise, functional skills, reasons for leaving jobs, etc., and from the answers provided, a pattern can be spotted.

4. Culture fit interviews:

This is the type of interview that I normally use. The crucial step here is to identify some of the positive behaviors a person needs to demonstrate and what would make the individual successful? It is important to have clear expectations of who would make an ideal candidate. Having gotten a list of the required qualities from the organization, one may ask very specific questions pertaining to the role and see if they are a match.

The other way of establishing cultural fit and correlating it is by leveraging psychometric instruments that determine motives, values, preferences, and more in an individual. As mentioned earlier, psychometric tests do not have a standardized format.

Hence, you will be able to manipulate it accordingly to derive the exact purpose you want from it. How may the individual behave in a specific situation or context? What are some of the values that drive them? These types of questions will point you toward the result. Another effective way is to conduct background and reference checks. This has to be done with openness and transparency and also by asking the right questions.

I have often seen highly capable people score exceedingly well in cognitive ability tests and have the relevant experience but fail or underperform frequently. Many candidates leave organizations in a short period, and others are asked to leave in a short period as well; the reason for this is they were not the right cultural fit for the organization. It is not a reflection of their capabilities; it is just that they were not the best fit for the team in terms of culture.

Whether for voluntary or involuntary reasons, losing a person is highly expensive for the organization. It can cost the organization 2-10 times the annual CTC of an individual, which includes both tangible and intangible costs. It may inevitably impact the reputation of the organization.

In terms of tools, over-reliance on any one tool builds in a certain amount of bias. Some measures can be undertaken to avoid this bias. Wherever possible, the organizations could leverage multiple tools and try to see a common pattern that emerges between the analyses of these various tools. This will most likely give you an accurate picture of the individual. Also, give importance to hiring the people with the right work experience and technical qualifications and people with the right positive attitude and values. When we talk about the right positive attitude, there are a few areas to look at:

    a) **The ability to learn and unlearn:** As discussed vaguely earlier, it is easy to become prisoners of our own experiences. Experiences are critical; they help you handle the situation better if you encounter similar circumstances.

    But you should not get accustomed to the understanding that experience is the only way to handle a situation. Experiences should not come at the cost of innovation. Sometimes you have to unlearn some old habits to make way for newer and more necessary elements.

b) **The orientation to accept something new:** As an extension of the previous point, it can be challenging to adapt to changes. Especially if someone has a lot of experience in a particular field, it can be difficult to accept the advances that might come their way, be it opinions, technology, or tools. One must be open to inviting new things into practice. A key trait to identify this behavior in someone is to see how open they are to trying new things.

c) **Orientation to question the status quo:** Traditional or conventional methods can be systematic and organized. This creates a comfort zone within which it is easy to get lost. In high-performing teams, we need people who defy conventional methods and think out of the box. To spot those individuals, you need to see if they exhibit qualities of assertiveness. Are they willing to question the usual ways in which things are done?

d) **The ability to be a collaborative team player:** Can they curb their desire for self-achievement and self-glory and be willing to be a part of the team which contributes and achieves the bigger goals? This is another area that we cover about attitude. Are they driven purely by financial goals? Or are they committed to a bigger purpose in the organization? Those who are driven purely by financial goals tend to take shortcuts. While this may achieve their short-term objectives, they do not necessarily create high-performing teams. This is a sign of disruptive behavior. They can become like a bull in a china shop and tend to introduce changes that do not align with the team or the organization. It is not endorsed, and it is rather destructive. It is important to challenge the status quo and do things differently, but it has to be done in a manner where change is aligned and communicated well. And a high-performing team can deliver and sustain that agenda.

The other tool I would like to talk about is the Lifeline Exercise. I call it such because one maps the positive experiences and not-so-positive experiences of one's life. The individual has a very open and honest conversation about his relevant past experiences.

I have found this to be very effective, especially when you are hiring leaders. Of course, we keep personal information confidential. The individual is allowed to share whatever he is comfortable sharing, and it is a safe space. We try to see the highs and lows of their lives.

We also look at some of the learnings they have been through due to those highs and lows. We try to see patterns. Patterns help us understand how a person copes under stress and pressure and also the person's ability to learn and unlearn.

This is indeed a powerful tool. But I will repeat the word of caution: Do not rely on one tool consistently. One has to use multiple tools and patterns to make the right choices. We also need to get various stakeholder interviews. There might be divergent views, which is fine. But what are the common, consistent views? That gives a fairly accurate picture of the individual. If there are divergent views, it is worth understanding. What are the reasons for these divergent views? How relevant and critical are those divergent views to the role the candidate will be performing in the organization? Based on these answers, one can make the right decision.

What is the impact of not hiring correctly? The more fundamental question would be, what comes in the way of not hiring correctly? We all have our own unconscious preferences. Like attracts like. People like to interact with people of similar personalities and similar thought processes, and these similarities might lead to unconscious bias. When hiring for high-performance teams, one looks at the diversity of talent. Here variety is based on meritocracy. We look at hiring people with diverse backgrounds and skillsets and integrating them to complement each skill set and thought process. This is a very important element in building high-performing teams. I have seen that it is better not to prescribe percentages or numbers based on traditional diversity stereotypes, which is a pitfall that many organizations fall into. But it is about creating a culture of meritocracy where hiring the right talent and building a high-performing team is all about hiring people with divergent skill sets. These divergent thought processes complement one another and bring in newer thinking. The role of the leader is very important as they have to manage this diversity.

They have to create the right environment. Organizations must attract the right kind of talent and maintain the environment to help them succeed. They need to hire candidates quickly. Sometimes, the cost of hiring a person too soon and hiring the wrong person is much higher than not hiring a person at all. I am not asking you to take your sweet time to hire, but just not to compromise on the quality of the candidate.

There is also a negative consequence in not building a high-performance structure. Word-of-mouth is especially potent in today's world.

If the word spreads that there is a political environment within an organization, it would be a harsh and long road back. I have seen several good organizations not attract the right talent and have a high drop-out ratio because they could not create the right environment.

Conceptually, the right environment promotes growth, considers the employees' mental and physical well-being, and has rewards in place to motivate them to achieve more. These are the challenges that come about while attracting the right people on board.

Let me talk about the importance of brand building when hiring talent. A lot of people like to work with a great brand. Candidates looking for a job are usually inclined toward well-known companies. But how exactly are great brands built? Ideally, if you ensure great products, a strong financial base, and regular awareness and communication, you are on your way to building a great brand if you have not already done so. There are times when organizations believe in underplaying their strengths and stress on humility. I agree with it conceptually.

However, it is important to position your brand in the external world via social media, print media, or television. This helps create awareness about what the organization stands for, what it delivers, and its vision. A great product also goes a long way in building the equity of an organization. Customer and employee feedback also matter, especially for employees who have left the organization. I have advised clients who do not have that large presence to source the right talent. One of the key things to note while building a brand's image is the candidate experience. Whether you are an unknown or well-known brand, the candidate's experience is critical. Every step counts from when the position is advertised to when a candidate is hired. Every step counts as each stage represents the organization.

Does the advertisement have clarity? Is it well-structured? Is all the necessary information given? Is the organization being transparent? And more. A well-structured, clear advertisement that provides all the pertinent information depicts how much effort the organization is willing to put into its employees.

Secondly, when candidates apply for a position, how are they handled? Is there a difference in the response sent to candidates whose CVs are approved and shortlisted compared to those sent to the candidates who did not make the cut? A long wait usually disengages the candidates and does not contribute to a great candidate experience.

Even if the candidate is not selected, the organization must get back to them and close the loop. Providing some sort of feedback to the candidates who are rejected is another way to help them. This will help them work on it and score another job. These are some simple ways to give back to the people to build trust between you and the world.

Thirdly, the way interviews are conducted goes a long way. Do they start and end on time? Is the candidate treated respectfully in the interview? Are the relevant questions asked? Is there a closure within the conversation in terms of the next steps? If the candidate is selected, how are they approached? How is the offer made? And how is the offer closed? Even if the candidate is keen on the job, everyone must keep their eyes open for red flags. The interview is your first encounter with a potential employee, so making the right first impression is mandatory. This will seal a factor of dedication from both sides starting from day one.

All these qualities matter while analyzing candidate experience. So, every phase of the entire hiring process, from the advertisement to choosing a candidate, contributes to developing the brand image. Even if the organization is not well-known, they will attract a crowd of the right candidates if they consistently provide a good candidate experience.

THE POWER OF NETWORKING AND THE LEADERSHIP ROLE IN ATTRACTING TALENT:

High-performing individuals work for organizations and also for their leaders. I have witnessed many high-performing teams disintegrating because of the lack of a good leader. A leader plays a very important role in presenting the brand image both externally and internally. Typically, one tends to imagine a leader as someone who guides or dictates, and the team follows accordingly. Such leadership may be one of the conventional ways to lead. But the definition of leadership is now evolving and more accommodating. The leader is entrusted with securing the work culture practices and creating a safe working environment. As a leader, you must understand the difference between being assertive and being a bully. A leader must practice giving and receiving feedback, provide constructive criticism to the team, and appreciate their efforts to create a safe environment.

As a leader, you might also have to anticipate your team's needs and try to meet them without them having to request it many times.

It could be on any issue from overworking, deadlines, salaries, etc. You can also cultivate deeper bonds by enquiring about their personal lives with genuine interest and making them feel welcome. A leader also interacts externally and internally, often. Apart from these things, there are other unsaid aspects that a leader must abide by, like being fair and impartial to the employees, promoting talent to take the lead, strictly avoiding any form of harassment, and providing adequate resources. Good leaders energize people who want to join their teams. I have seen many cases in my career where lesser-known organizations have attracted talent without offering great salaries. The only reason candidates join these teams is because of their good candidate experience orchestrated by excellent leaders. Such leaders will, without a doubt, impart their passion to their team members as well. This is the reason why they are willing to work with that particular organization and its leaders. These teams eventually transform into great businesses, and the leaders could attract the best possible talent.

HOW DO YOU SOURCE THE RIGHT TALENT?

1) Internal references are a good way to hire people, but we must ensure they undergo the same interview process and are selected on merit.

2) Leveraging head hunters. Engage the right executive search firm. Ensure that the firm understands your business and work culture. The firm must be aware of the kind of candidates you want. These may not necessarily be big search firms. I have witnessed many not-so-famous firms give far more effective results than well-established firms. It is all about the consultant understanding your business and the profile you are looking at and making an effort to source them right. The consultant must be able to sell your story to the organization.

3) Another effective source is advertising on job sites or social media sites like LinkedIn, and maybe even on Facebook or Instagram. These are also good ways of reaching out and connecting.

The level of engagement is heightened on these sites. I have been able to attract and hire some best talents via LinkedIn. Some were not even looking for a position actively.

The key is to look at profiles that match the job requirements and start a conversation. Regular advertisements also work, be it in papers or on social media. I mentioned Instagram and Facebook earlier.

Even though they are not the go-to sites for job postings, you might find interesting results through networking. People do have the option to share their posts on these sites, which is why you might be able to reach a larger audience if executed properly. Nowadays, printing on paper has gone off practice.

However, keep that option open. You might end up getting some really good candidates. Another option is participating in large forums, where organizations can interact with people, build a network, and attract talent. This provides an opportunity to give the audience a tour of your organization and explain to a wider crowd who you are. It has the potential to bring you more candidates.

Let us consider two case studies to better understand the importance of hiring.

CASE STUDY 1:

This is a case study about an organization that was able to attract good talent. An established organization used a particular strategy to build a high-performing team by attracting the right talent. The organization was a global market leader in the technology sector. They were setting up their global services in India.

They were planning to start from a team of 200-300 and scale up to 15,000 over a period of time. For this mission to succeed, they needed the right set of leaders. The key part was to attract the best leaders who could lead in the transformation and growth of the company. So, the company started its hiring process. The CEO was in place, and the CEO hired a competent HR head. The role of the head of HR was to act as the brand ambassador of the company. So almost 60% of the head of HR's time was spent in talent acquisition to build a strong team under him/her to attract the best possible talent. They used all the available resources to make this happen. Recruitment process firms were contacted. Posts were put on LinkedIn.

Executive search consultants were brought in, and employee references were taken into account, and they also looked in their own network. These were all various approaches in terms of sourcing the right talent. Obviously, a lot of time was spent on this process. The first hiring was executed successfully at the leadership level. They got the vertical business and functional heads in place.

The first task given to them was to create an organizational structure, which would not only be for that year but could also be continued for another three to four years. The recruits carried on with their tasks. The company then hired the right number of people in a phased manner, as per the approved business plan. For the first three years, 50%–60% of the leadership team's time was spent building high-performing teams.

KEY CHALLENGES FACED:

1. It is getting the right kind of people. Because when it comes to hiring volumes, there is a possibility of compromising on the right talent. The recruitment process had to be strong.
2. Individuals were being hired in a fairly good market. The organization had to make sure that the candidate joined their team once the offer was made. The drop-out ratio was high. So, the entire candidate experience had to be positive in the interview. The whole team took a lot of due diligence and care (HR and the business team.). They also made competitive offers in the 66th percentile of the market.
3. They were looking at the right kind of skills. There was a lot of focus on the skills in the initial hiring stage. They were only looking for people who were capable of doing their current job. That said, one-third of the team was hired for potential.
4. The right hiring process and tools were introduced. Psychometrics and competency-based interviews were used, and the teams and managers were trained in these tools proactively.
5. All managers had consistent work performance.
6. They were trained to have a consistent view by identifying the right positive and contradictory performance.
7. From the time the candidate was made an offer and hired, the organization was quick and fast in the decision-making process. There were no more than four rounds of interviews. The experience was designed to be the least cumbersome for the candidate.

This was done to ensure that they acquired proper talent for the organization and the right leaders were hired and empowered to make decisions. Candidate experience was graded 4.5 on a 5-point scale.

This also helped get references from candidates. In fact, there were candidates who did not get a job but referred many candidates as they liked the candidate experience. All these factors helped the organization attract the right talent. Most of them came from a technical background, and they joined the company even though they were only paid average salaries. What made them join? Well, the engagement with the leaders and the organization made them want to work for that organization.

We see how much time and effort was spent initially on creating good leaders. This process ensures that the companies are patient enough to put enough effort to acquire a good team, therefore establishing the importance of their employees. So, this way, a 200–300-member team scaled up to a 15,000-member team. Several leaders in the organization were active speakers in the industry forums and put up a dynamic representation of their organization. This also built a lot of positive visibility and attracted good talent for the company.

CASE STUDY 2: START-UP

This is about a start-up where mistakes were made in terms of building a high-performance team. One particular challenge was hiring the right kind of talent to join their team and having the right mix (Experienced and fresh talent; the blend of experience and youth).

A start-up approached me as they were facing issues in performance, and on analysis, these were the causes I found: There was no defined organizational structure. They did not have the right kind of spans, layers, and hierarchy. So, while start-ups are usually flat organizations, a certain hierarchy is needed to ensure the right blend of experience at individual and managerial levels. It would mean that the founder does not have to get involved with every transactional activity. The founder, in this case, was a highly capable individual with the ability to think strategically and a strong commercial orientation.

This particular start-up had a good idea and a good product. It also boasted of a good network and good technology and, as a result, had attracted a lot of business. But I was consulted due to the direct involvement of the entrepreneur. During the initial stages, an entrepreneur has to be extremely hands-on. But when it comes down to the actual delivery and scale-up of the organization, the company needs to have the right organizational structure and the right level of talent support to go along with its growth strategy.

So, the gap in creating high-performance teams was first in terms of structure. The strategy was clear and defined; they had no problems on this count. However, in terms of the organizational structure, individual contributors were either freshers or one to two years into their careers; they were hired to deliver analytical solutions.

There can be a misconception that hiring from tier 1 and tier 2 colleges can guarantee the right talent. However, the key objective here is to hire people who have the hunger, enthusiasm, and passion for delivering and growing their careers with the organization. It is especially important with a start-up.

In this case, the managerial team consisted of people who had no experience in managerial roles. They were appointed as first-time managers purely because they were highly experienced, individual contributors. They were not trained effectively in people management skills. Consequently, the performance delivery started suffering. There were pockets of individual brilliance, but they could not collaborate across roles and boundaries as a team. They did not get the right kind of support from the managers in defining clear performance standards, coaching and mentoring, or timely feedback.

Because of these reasons, they were not able to deliver value to the clients' expectations. So, the first thing we did was train the managers. How could they become effective managers and subsequently individual contributors? How do they become team players? While we were conducting the initial diagnosis, it was found that training was given importance. But training in itself without context will only serve a limited purpose. Therefore, we had to correct the organizational structure, define the right skills, and have clear job descriptions for each role. We also worked toward having the right spans and layers.

We brought forth mid-level manager roles so that the CEO/founder did not have to spend a disproportionate amount of time managing individual contributors. We created the right kind of spans and layers. We introduced a layer where a manager could guide first-time managers. We did not hire too many and only recruited three people who could add value to that role. Their role was to ensure that the managers were equipped to handle the operational and tactical issues. We knew we had to start by first hiring right. We also invested in developing the managers' people management skills, which included three parts:

a. Managing self – How do they plan? How do they organize themselves? How do they prioritize? How do they manage their time effectively?
b. Managing others – How do they handle conflict? How do they influence and inspire their team? How do they coach and develop their team? How do they motivate the team?
c. Managing business – How do they manage performance in terms of creating performance goals? How to appraise and evaluate performance? How to give performance feedback? How to reward and recognize performance? How to manage their top performers and underperformers?

Having addressed this holistically, we found that, both at a structural and development level, the net promoter score grew by three points after a year, and the customer satisfaction (on a scale of 1–5) went up from 2.75 to 4.5.

Our learnings from this case were as follows:
    a. By doing simple remedial steps, you can create the right structure with the right spans and layers.
    b. Invest in training and developing the team.
    c. Ensure that you hire the right personnel.

In this case, the hiring methods were wrong. Their line managers were not trained. They had just two rounds of interviews. So, there was an investment in enhancing their hiring process via leveraging tools like psychometric tools, cognitive ability tests, and technical case studies, where people could go through that online. They were screened based on these tests before going into personal interviews. It saved time and improved hiring efficiency. It also reduced the overall cost of hiring. Line managers were put through interviewing skills workshops where they were trained in behavioral interviewing techniques, asking the right questions, interpreting the response correctly to be more consistent in the way they looked at candidates.

So, this improved the overall consistency of hiring and ensured that they could bring the right talent into the organization and create a talent pipeline for the future. In doing so, they kept the salaries at a market median level. They did not have to pay exorbitant money. I have seen a lot of start-ups with huge funding.

They end up paying disproportionate salaries to hire candidates; as a result, the business does not grow to the same level.

The burnout both in terms of the bottom-line and the people burnout is very high in such cases. This was a classic case where a start-up enhanced its recruitment process to hire the right kind of people. That is how they could build high-performing teams; by correcting their organizational structure and creating effective learning and development practices.

TAKEAWAYS:

- Hire people with complementary skills—work toward maintaining diversity in terms of skills and thought processes.
- Hire at least one-third of your team with a focus on potential along with the right experience.
- Ensure that you can create a very positive candidate experience for the people who apply to your organization.
- Ensure that you consider an individual's 'culture fit' element while hiring.
- Focus on building your brand, both organizational and leadership. Enhancing this will make candidates want to work for you.
- Permit enough time to source for the right set of leaders. The right set of leaders will have no trouble navigating their team forward.
- On the same note, any mistake made on a leadership level may cost you a lot of time and money.

6

DEVELOPING TALENT TO CREATE A HIGH PERFORMING TEAM

"Teamwork is the ability to work together towards a common vision. The ability to direct individual accomplishments toward organizational objectives. It is the fuel that allows common people to attain uncommon results."

- Andrew Carneige

The above quote clearly points to the importance of teams. I would like to tell you the story of Joseph Priestly. He was a brilliant amateur scientist, flourishing during 1765. He was later recognized as one of the first scientists to independently discover oxygen, a discovery that changed everything in the world of chemistry. Priestley's life-changing moments occurred when he visited the Club of Honest Whigs, an informal group highly associated with Benjamin Franklin.

It was a small club full of great minds who got together a couple of times in a week to discuss science, religion, politics, and more. It is said that Priestly, who visited the club to get feedback on a book idea, was met with much enthusiasm by Benjamin and his friends, who mentored and supported him with resources, such as a private library.

They allowed him to explore his ideas fully and provided him with feedback and support. In fact, Benjamin Franklin is known for encouraging talent and passion in others with his guidance and support. This is a valuable story because, while it sounds like just another club, it was in some way a team that worked to bring the best in each other.

These men gathered to share thoughts and ideas that have brought a noticeable change in their careers as individuals. The 'Club' produced more than one brilliant individual. It was a high-performing team, through and through.

We have discussed in the previous chapters the value a high-performing team can bring to the table. There is no doubt that the best teams are the ones that can yield the highest performance. There are many ways to create or build a high-performing team. However, it is a gradual process and involves a series of steps that are required to polish and bring out the best in every member.

A proven element that makes this process easier is to first really know and understand your employees' characteristics, strengths, and weaknesses. Every individual has their distinguishable features, and each person's field of interest and caliber definitely varies. In an organization, there are various levels of employment, and each of them carries a different set of roles.

If the roles are assigned without properly knowing the employees, then there are high chances that you have misplaced them in the wrong sector. We understand that in a team, there are a lot of different responsibilities, and assigning the responsibility to the right person is indeed a big factor in building a high-performance team.

Say, for example, handing an intellectual process to a professionally hired person based on technical skills and entrusting the technical side to a person who is good with intellectual ability would definitely complicate things.

Would you rather have these people invest time in learning a new skill from scratch or spend sufficient time in the beginning and associate each employee to match their strengths? The choice is yours. However, remember that only the right choices will develop a high-performing team. n this chapter, we will explore some methods that contribute highly to building a team that is high-performing.

It is no secret that the world today is changing every second. There is something new in the world every day that deserves to be on the headline. Such a transforming world almost demands us to change with it.

The ideas, foundations, and different methods that worked previously might not necessarily work well now. We could not have imagined that we would wake up to a pandemic one day. The pandemic, in fact, is a great example to understand how quickly the world adapts and moves on. On that note, it is important to understand how important it is for development itself to adapt and evolve, and second, how development strategies and methodologies have changed through the years.

Let us understand how development works by exploring a few case studies. There are three case studies that I would like to share about creating high-performance teams. Let us start with a large global multinational corporation I have been associated with for over five years. This corporate had earlier invested a lot in the development of their employees. But the strategies changed with a change in leadership. Any initiated development always brought some sort of a positive outcome, but at the same time, it was not really being taken to a conclusive level. There was no clear path from the initiation of the development or intervention to culmination and transition into the scaling of the workforce. Workforce typically includes all levels, including the individual contributors, the managerial levels, and the leadership and senior management teams. Therefore, to ensure that there is consistency and stability, keeping in mind that there is also an opportunity to revisit the changing skill requirements of the entire global workforce, very structured learning, and development strategy was created.

The strategy was focused on identifying career paths, wherein career paths typically address a person who joins as an individual contributor. An individual could opt for the two probable workstreams are the technical career framework and managerial or leadership framework. It highlights some of the vertical and horizontal moves a person needs to make. It also spoke about

1. What kind of formal qualifications or certifications are required?
2. What kind of work experience does one require?
3. What kind of external and internal training programs does one need?
4. Where can one leverage coaching and mentoring support?
5. What kind of projects could a person take?
6. What kind of job experiences should a person have to be considered eligible for the next move, either in the technical workstream or in the managerial stream?

The framework tests the rich job experience and the skills and capabilities of an individual before they are moved to the next level. We started by creating a career framework and then moved on to creating a competency framework. A model that broadly describes performance excellence within an organization is called the competency framework. Such a framework usually includes a number of competencies that are applied to multiple occupational roles within the organization. Each competency in generic terms defines excellence in working behavior.

Thus, a competency framework becomes highly relevant. The competency framework also enables the employees to have a clear understanding of the behaviors to be exhibited and the levels of performance that are to be expected in order to achieve organizational results. Then came the question of assessing what kind of technical skills, technical knowledge, or functional knowledge is required. What kind of leadership skills and soft skills does one need? It threw some light on some of the behavioral indicators: positive behavioral indicators and negative behavioral indicators.

Behavioral indicators definitely play a huge part in the assessment of an individual. For example, if you were to assess competency in the criterion "manages conflict well," the actual competency should be clearly defined to ensure that all assessors or observers fully understand it. We would need to produce a list of positive and negative behavioral indicators for this competency. Positive and negative behavioral indicators definitely highlight what a person needs to do to be successful for the current role and the next role. It can be considered quite an exhaustive exercise.

The first step was ascertaining the career path. We then move on to the competency path as the next step. The competency path can be an indicator across all levels. It helps you understand the knowledge skills and the right behavioral attributes and identify the kind of experiences you need to consider before moving to the next level? We highly customized it instead of going with the generic leadership competency framework. To define leadership competencies are leadership skills and behaviors that contribute to superior performance.

By using a competency-based approach in coaching, organizations or institutes can better identify the areas of improvement. Then, people were assessed on these customized skills. We had to find out whether or not they had the skills.

So, it was leveraging a combination of cognitive ability tests and technical and functional skills and tests. There were assessments and development centers for assessing the leadership skills of individuals. Based on the assessments, the strengths and the gaps of individuals were identified, and individual development plans for bridging these gaps were created. These plans were simple and only ran to a couple of pages at the most. All these steps were a part of the individual development plan. One focused on leveraging the 70:20:10 model. This means that 70% of a person's learning happens on the job through challenging and stretched assignments. Eighty percent of an individual's learning happens through coaching and mentoring both internally and externally, and 10% happens through attending formal training programs, reading, self-learning, formal education, etc.

So, a blended and integrated approach to learning was followed to attain the 70:20:10 model. This mainly helped in

(i) ensuring that the entire learning was sustainable,
(ii) ensuring that it was relevant to the individual
(iii) creating the right outcomes and measures for the organizations.

Many organizations do not get the equation right in terms of learning and development. I think learning and development are not related to the business strategy. The strategy is often growth, but you are developing individuals to do a good maintenance job; it does not necessarily correlate. There should be sufficient input from the management to enable employees to look into their ability to manage growth, work with ambiguity, work at a fast pace, and execute and implement strategies effectively. Another place where employees get stuck in their development journey is when the development is intervention-based and not linked to the desired outcome or an unrealistic desired outcome.

I would like to share here the example of a large organization that embarked on a coaching program. The leadership team was unclear about the deliverables before they engaged an external coach. The external coach was just expected to have random-once-in-a-quarter discussions with a leadership team member.

It did serve a purpose; there were no clear, measurable outcomes where one could assess whether coaching was helping the organization in any way; there were no qualitative measures.

Although it was a well-intended move, the organization did not sufficiently leverage the coach because the objectives were not clearly defined. Objectives are a very important part of any organization, especially when it comes to coaching. Objectives provide a basis for planning and for developing other types of plans. They act as motivators for individuals and departments of an enterprise, such as a coaching institute. Sound objectives eliminate haphazard action, which may result in undesirable consequences.

They also facilitate coordinated behavior of the various groups who otherwise may pull in different directions. Since the objectives were not clear enough, the deliverables were not defined clearly. A third area where organizations fail to get it right is sustainability.

Sustainability in learning and skill development is not a one-off journey. Very often, organizations feel that they have done enough by investing in a two-day or three-day classroom training program and expect returns at the end. But ideally, a person has to be taken through the process until there are observable changes in behavior or skills. The role of the individual becomes very important here because they have to be willing to learn. Like I had mentioned earlier, you can take a horse to the water, but you cannot make it drink. People have to be self-motivated to want to learn and acquire those skills and experiences. Also, the line manager has to support the individual by creating and enabling the right kind of blocks and the right kind of support and sponsorship. And finally, the organization also needs to attain some of the key measures of success and define them in a very clear manner. Keep in mind that all measures of success will not be quantitative; some will be qualitative.

Another area where organizations go wrong is not knowing the right methodology to invest in and often going by the flavor of the day. For example, I have come across people wanting to do a course on design thinking or people wanting to do a course on OKR. I ask them a simple question, "What problem are you trying to solve?"

They often do not have clear answers about the problem they want to solve. And even when they do, the methodology they choose has no link to the problem which they are trying to solve. It is very important to know what a person is trying to do; having a sound plan is very necessary.

Planning minimizes risk and uncertainty by providing a more rational, fact-based procedure for making decisions, and planning allows managers and organizations to minimize risk and uncertainty.

Planning also leads to success, although it does not guarantee success. Studies have shown that all things being equal, companies that plan outperform the non-planners and their past results. Often people hear of some flavor of the day or activity; they read about it, and they like it, and so they try to force-fit that solution into a strategy.

I think development starts by helping organizations, whether they are social, political, or military organizations, achieve their strategic goals by developing people's capabilities. Organizations facilitate the pattern of communication. They also help in locating decision centers to create proper balance, and most importantly, they stimulate creativity and encourage growth. So, if we are able to get these equations right, I think we will be able to achieve a good measure of success.

DEVELOPMENT METHODOLOGIES:

Classroom training/Virtual training: The first development methodology that I will explain is traditional classroom training or virtual training. Classroom training or virtual training is about a facilitator transferring knowledge, leveraging a variety of approaches and techniques like lectures, case studies, role-plays, experiential learning exercises or activities, and business simulations; moreover, a lot of facilitators are also leveraging outbound learning experiences.

Instructor-led training is effective when it comes to building interaction between participants, addressing real-time queries, and immediate transfer of knowledge.

One possible disadvantage of in-classroom training is that it is facilitator enabled, especially when it comes to experimental learning, and there may be inconsistencies in how training is delivered across multiple locations. The approaches to teaching vary from person to person. The way it is taught by one faculty might not be the same in the next classroom. While the different approaches are not necessarily a problem from the teaching perspective, they could still result in inconsistencies that may affect the rate at which one reaches the goal. Cultural nuances, such as linguistic barriers, may also come in the way of effective instructor-led training.

Instructor-led training needs to be complemented with job coaching and mentoring to ensure that the knowledge acquired in a classroom training session is applied on the job.

Failing this, until and unless a person is highly self-motivated, which is true for only a very small percentage of the population, maybe 1% to 2%, most would not make a conscious effort to apply their learnings on the job.

COACHING: We will talk about coaching in detail in the upcoming chapters. However, I would like to briefly introduce it as it is one of the most effective methodologies.

There are a few types of coaching:

- **Executive coaching** is meant to facilitate professional and personal development to the point of individual growth, improved performance, and contentment. It deals specifically with the unique set of challenges created from crossing cultures. It deals with the difficulties in attaining professional goals amidst a changing political and social structure while dealing with an individual's unique social and personal hurdles. Here the coach works with the individuals to solve their issues, problems, or challenges faced in the workplace, presently or in the past, mainly related to business. Business Coaching is a highly effective methodology, and it can be done on a one-to-one or one-to-many basis. This is a highly effective method because it provides customized and focused solutions that aid in improving and enhancing an individual's performance both in the current job as well as in future jobs.

- **Life coaching** is about helping people to determine and achieve personal goals. A coach will use a variety of methods customized to the needs of his pupil. It helps individuals address their personal challenges and create a smart action plan. It allows one to address their life goals, be it financial goals, emotional goals, relationship goals, well-being goals, social goals, or spiritual goals.

- **Organization development coaching** enables a coach to work with large or small groups of people within an organization.
  It helps address a strategy and enables the achievement of strategic goals such as growth, restructuring, change in strategy, introducing new technology, introducing a new project, or looking at a new market differently.
  These are the areas where organizations play an important role in addressing their business needs.

Overall, coaching is an effective way of giving the right results and outcomes and measuring success. One area where organizations need to be careful is being clear about their objectives. One needs to ask the right questions. Why are you engaging a coach? Often coaching does not work or is unnecessary because the manager could have addressed the same issue by one or two feedback sessions. If it requires somebody externally or internally to be working with the individual on a sustained basis for at least a period of six months to a year, then it is worth engaging a coach. It is important to make the right decision. Strictly speculate whether there is a need for an internal coach or an external coach.

MENTORING: Moving on to the third methodology, we have Mentoring. Mentoring is about uplifting by an experienced individual who can be a sounding board, friend, philosopher, and guide. The mentoring relationship should be based on trust, confidentiality, mutual respect, and sensitivity.

- The relationship should be based on agreed boundaries and ground rules that address the power differentials between the mentor and mentee. A mentor should be a person who is qualified to advise an individual on what he needs to do.
- Mentoring is a relatively unstructured process. But yes, organizations are putting together structured mentoring programs where individuals can catch up with their mentors on a regular basis. Of course, they catch up on some of the key points discussed earlier whilst maintaining confidentiality.
- The mentors note the key takeaways for the mentee from the session and get across what the mentee needs to be doing. Even though the words coaching and mentoring are used as if they were synonymous with each other, there is an absolute difference between a coach and a mentor.
- Coaching and mentoring do exist for the same purpose: to help others grow, develop, and reach their full potential. But one of the key elements of mentoring, if done in a proper way, is the potential for the relationship to last a lifetime.

  Typically mentoring is voluntary, whether the mentoring takes place informally through personal networks or formally through a company mentoring program. The role of a mentor is to listen, learn, and advise.

- On the other hand, a coach can make us understand life better, improve our mindset, and equip us with skills to handle future challenges and situations. Compared with mentoring, coaching is typically more structured and tailored to specific outcomes than general personal development. This more formal structure is also because coaches charge for their services, unlike mentors.

VIRTUAL LEARNING: Finally, we have virtual learning. Virtual Learning has emerged as a very powerful way of sharing information which is very similar to instructor-led learning. Here, an instructor delivers sessions virtually, and the content can be very similar but with additional features like breakout rooms and whiteboard discussions to ensure that interactivity does not get lost in virtual learning sessions.

A few words of caution are really important for virtual meetings.

- Virtual meeting sessions should not exceed 2-3 hours. Three hours is the maximum it should go because there will be participation fatigue and screen fatigue.
- Try to give breaks every one hour and fifteen minutes or every one and a half hours. Such breaks after every session, especially considering that it is a virtual learning session, will help people unwind and take time out from staring at the screen. While virtual learning is advertised as something that is comfortable, in reality, it can be very strenuous on the eyes.
- Virtual learning sessions require participants to be highly engaged. A lot of them would be off-camera, so it is not possible for facilitators to see the audience here.
- In such a scenario, a facilitator could introduce some interactive activities every 10 to 15 minutes to break the fatigue of continuously listening to the facilitator.

  These activities could be as simple as games, business simulations, case studies, or role plays, or something as basic as the facilitator asking questions every 15 minutes just to keep a check.

E-LEARNING: E-learning is a very effective way of transferring knowledge, and it can be a very powerful way of ensuring consistent delivery of information. It is very effective in areas like compliance training; that is, only knowledge transfer is required.

E-learning is very useful in product training. However, E-learning does not necessarily result in skill-building. E-learning can also be used as a complementary activity, which can be undertaken either before or after instructor-led training. It is very beneficial in a blended learning program. I have seen a number of organizations, especially large organizations, use it for product training, compliance training, and in training for certain soft skills to complement the instructor-led training programs. Even though the initial investment is higher in E-learning, eventually, especially when organizations are looking at large volumes over diverse areas, it turns out to be very cost-effective.

Today, a number of E-learning packages are also mobile-enabled, which makes it easier for people to access them. Another method is through business simulations or gamification, where the entire learning is put through a virtual gamification experience. This helps not only to learn, but people promote gamification for assessment centers. It definitely has its advantages, but I personally feel that a case study facilitates discussions based on it. Whether it is a case study or gamification, it is the quality of discussions that follow, which help you in areas like problem-solving, decision making, and strategic thinking.

One can also see the impact of a person's thinking and decisions on outcomes on the ground. I will share an example of leveraged gamification tied up with global gamification, which is used in assessment centers to assess senior executives' strategic thinking change and management decision-making abilities. Here it was about a pharmaceutical company, and one could see the impact of the decisions on the organization's stock price. There was a visible result in terms of employee engagement—seen in terms of the overall profitability of the business as well as the impact on market share. It is important to realize that while all these methods provide give a good simulated environment, they cannot be used in isolation and have to be facilitated by an instructor or coach.

As we are nearing the end of this chapter, I would like to address Action Learning products. Now, typically these are attained after instructor-led training or e-learning or gamification, knowing that there has been effective knowledge transfer. This provides an opportunity for participants to apply their learning through real-life projects in the workplace or beyond and translate that learning into skills. This can be done either in terms of real-life or business projects within the organization. People can work in cross-functional or similar teams, or they may take up external projects outside the organization, especially for products involving work with a social sector.

Personally, having worked in the social sector, I can see a lot of potential work there. It is a great opportunity for people to transfer their knowledge and convert it into skills both within the organization and without in the external sector. People have to go through classroom learning, virtual learning, eLearning courses, coaching, or mentoring for hidden talent to emerge. When one is allowed to participate in actual learning projects, it is always good to have an internal or external mentor who facilitates this entire learning process.

Ideally, a combination of an internal and an external mentor is helpful. While an external person brings an outside view or perspective, an internal mentor is available to ensure that all the needs from the organization's side are met as and when required. I cannot emphasize enough how powerful it is to learn on the job. To ensure this happens, give the individual challenging tasks and assignments. Let the individual have an internal mentor or an external coach to help them navigate through these challenges. There is no better way to learn than from life and experience; you learn swimming only by getting into the water. However, when you are effectively coached or trained, you will be able to swim successfully and safely. The risk and the impact both to the organization and the individual are minimized. This is a far better approach than pushing a person into the water, knowing that they may sink. Remember, if they sink, there is a high chance that they will pull you down as well.

TAKEAWAYS:

- Performing teams can only achieve their greatest level of collective impact when they have an effective layer. We discussed various layers or constraints that need to be followed to build a very effective, high-performing team.
- There are various methodologies that can be followed, and choosing the right one that fits the situation is the most important thing; the methodologies might vary from person to person.
- Organizations need to maintain business continuity, whatever the situation might be. Adapting to any circumstance is also a survival skill. The need for high-performing teams has increased with the advent of new technologies, especially with the challenge of managing costs and adding new services.

- There has been a significant amount of research about what makes a great team and how organizations can use this knowledge to build high-performing teams. Interestingly, it is reported that only 10% to 20% of the teams rank themselves as high-performing teams; so, there is clearly an opportunity for leaders, coaches, and mentors to step up.
- Developing clarity, accountability, better decision-making, trust, and communication will boost the chances of becoming a high-performing team.

7

RETAINING & SUSTAINING HIGH PERFORMANCE

"Employees who are engaged are more likely to stay with their organization, reducing overall turnover and the costs associated with it. They feel a stronger bond to their organization's mission and purpose, making them more effective brand ambassadors. They build stronger relationships with customers, helping their company increase sales and profitability."
— The Gallup 2017 State of the American Workplace report

RETAINING HIGH PERFORMANCE

We have discussed how attracting and developing high performers is vital for an organization's success. However, it is not good enough if you attract and develop high performers but later see them leave to other organizations. An equally crucial aspect of company growth is the retention of high performers.

So, how to retain the high performers?

The one seemingly obvious answer is by giving them a higher remuneration. But is it the right answer?

However, as the quote from the 2017 Gallup report on the American workplace suggests, you need an engaged workforce and not necessarily the most highly-paid workforce. The report even quantifies the importance of a highly engaged workforce. It reveals that *highly engaged business units achieve a 10% increase in customer metrics and a 20% increase in sales*. So, the question here is, how to keep the high-performing workforce engaged?

The first step is to understand the key motivators. Why do people stay and contribute to high-performing teams? The first aspect is that they develop a sense of purpose. This purpose goes beyond their job description and key result areas. They know that they are contributing to a bigger purpose, and they are doing a meaningful job in driving team performance and business performance. The Gallup report also cites the importance of purpose for the employees. It states- *"Employees want to feel good about their organization and what it offers the world. They want to be able to say, 'I like what this company stands for.' If employees do not believe in their company or do not believe that the company can successfully uphold its brand or reputation, they are prone to look for a different job."*

One of the ways to build purpose within the organization is to have clear, defined goals or key deliverables that connect with the personal goals and objectives of the employees. In the absence of a clearly defined goal or key expectations or key deliverables and success measures, teams tend to lose their focus and a sense of purpose which will later fail to create high performance.

A clear reward system constitutes the second crucial aspect of retaining the high-performers. Remuneration may not be the most important element in retaining high performers, but on the same note, it cannot be ignored. The urge to work harder multiplies magnanimously as the employees realize that their effort is going to be appreciated, whether through remuneration or public acknowledgment or award. High-performers must feel rewarded for their efforts to stay at the top of their game. Rewards often come in two forms- financial and non-financial. Financial rewards are reflected in annual increments, bonuses, long-term incentives plans (LTIPs), and employee stock options (ESOPs). Non-financial rewards can take the form of recognition through awards, internally or externally. Some organizations provide an opportunity for high-performers to represent the organization on speaker forums. High-performers often feel more valued when they are considered thought leaders.

When appreciated by their leaders, senior managers, and even clients, they are encouraged for their endeavors. Later in the chapter, we shall explore the various means and ways of rewarding high performers.

The third crucial aspect of retaining a high performance is having a clear and planned career growth path. Remuneration is never the full-stop for any career-oriented, high-performing employee. They always seek growth while working for any organization. A cohesion between organizational goals and individual goals is necessary for any high-performing employee. The organization's human resource department must include a chart of career growth for every prospective employee. Gurus of organizational behavior have predicted that if an organization provides planned career growth to the employees, even an average performer can transform into a high-performer. Now, which steps can reflect career growth? It can be like, initiating some innovative and exciting projects, challenging assignments, global exposure, including the employees in the strategic decision-making process of the organizations, etc.

The key motivators that help any business grow shall also help in individualistic growth. Developing personal connection nurtures another critical aspect of retaining high performers. Organizations must foster and build a personal connection with their high-performing teams. High-performing teams are intended to perform, and they perform better when their strengths are valued. They must be allowed to contribute. And it is imperative to provide them with a collaborative environment where they can utilize the cumulative strength of each other while solving business problems. So, how do you build such an environment?

You build a collaborative environment by fostering different types of connections at various levels. The team leader must build a cordial relationship with each team member. Similarly, each member should engage in a good rapport with one another. It can be done via formal events like reviews, meetings, and even informal events like social events, get-togethers, potluck lunches, or dinners. It is imperative to build a healthy relationship beyond the transactional nature of work.

ROLE OF MANAGER IN RETAINING HIGH PERFORMING TALENT:

A manager plays an important role in retaining high-performing talent.

It starts with keeping clear goals and linking those goals with the organization's business objectives. A clear goal sets an organization's mission and imparts the various modes to attain the goal.

It indeed emphasizes the reason behind the set goal, for without providing a valid justification for the goal, employees can never be motivated to perform. It helps the organization relate to each individual's goals and establish the interdependence of individual goals. Such interdependence ensures that the team goals are aligned with the team members' goals and contribute towards a common cause.

A manager must evaluate and review performances while implementing clear evaluating performance measures. A distinctive outline must define the following points: What does it mean to exceed performance? What does it mean to achieve the expected level of performance? What defines underperformance?

Several approaches are available to measure performance. Some organizations follow a 5-point scale. The scale goes from 1-5, where 1 indicates poor performance; 2 indicates the need for improvement; 3 signifies that the performance has met expectations.

A score of 4 reflects upon a performance that exceeds expectation, while 5 is given to outstanding performances. In the case of the 4-point scale of measuring performance: 1 - needs improvement, 2 - meets expectations, 3 - exceeds expectations, 4- outstanding.

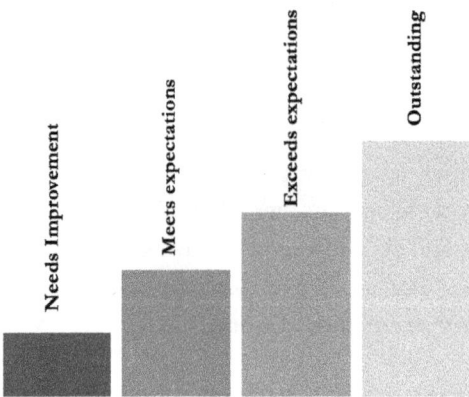

Then, there are some organizations that follow a 3-point scale to measure levels of performance. 1 is given for the performance that doesn't meet expectations, while 2 is for those who consistently meet the expectations, and 3 marks the exceeding the expectations.

I am a profound believer in the 3-point model. The rest of the models are ways and means of finding justifications for fitting performance measurement into a bell curve of performance. However, performance is fairly tangible; either one consistently meets performance expectations or doesn't meet them consistently.

And the third possibility is to exceed the expectations. The 3-point model does not entertain the shades of in-between, which is about finding a way of force-fitting or manipulating the performance information. Statistically, performance is tangible. This evaluation reflects the 'what' part of the performance, i.e., the achievement of the performance against the key result areas. Another significant aspect revolves around the 'how' part of the performance. It is reflected through the behavior of the person while achieving the performance.

People also leverage a competency framework and measure a person on the 'how' part of the performance. Employees are often measured through their problem-solving skills, sense of innovation, decision-making skills, adapting ability to changes, managing conflict, and strategic thinking for the employees of the senior levels. Amongst the various competency frameworks, every organization has a different perspective while deciding on the framework that works for them.

Organizations also look at other softer attributes like operational excellence, the ability to work independently without constant supervision, the ability to drive long-term benefits instead of short-term gains as they evaluate the 'why' part of the performance. I have seen people who achieve (technically) or may overachieve the 'what' part of the performance. However, while scrutinizing the 'why' part of the performance, we may end up finding the individual underperforming.

Usually, at the entry levels or the junior management levels, about 70-80% weightage is given to the 'what' part of the performance, and 20% is prescribed for the 'why' part. At the mid-management levels, 60% weightage is given to the 'what' part and 40% on the 'why' part of the performance. At the senior management levels, the weightage is equally divided between the 'what' and 'why' parts of the performance. This weightage is crucial because if you get the 'why' right at senior management levels, you can also get the 'what' part delivered.

With my experience, I feel 60% weightage should be assigned to the 'why' part of the performance and 40% to the 'what' part of the performance.

As per the Gallup report:

"Highly engaged organizations share common philosophies and practices. For example, they know that engagement starts at the top. Their leaders are aligned in prioritizing engagement as a competitive, strategic point of differentiation.

They communicate openly and consistently. They place the utmost importance on using the right metrics and hiring and developing great managers. Highly engaged organizations also hold their managers accountable — not just for their team's measured engagement level, but also for how it relates to their team's overall performance."

SUSTAINING HIGH PERFORMANCE:

"Success comes through sustained effort."- Todd Brison:

As we learned the various strategies and methodologies essential for creating and developing a high-performing team, we realized that the key challenge does not crop up while building, developing, and nurturing a high-performing team but in maintaining consistency in the performance. Maintenance is a difficult task that comes at the cost of persistence.

The effort must be consistent in the direction of your dreams. The keyword here is not *effort* but *sustained.* Sustaining a team is of greater importance when it comes to building a high-performing team. Consistency is essential for establishing and maintaining high-performing production teams.

Consistency is indeed a hard concept to practice. If one is asked to try something 50 times to make it through finally, hesitation would be the first reaction which can even lead to withdrawal from the task altogether.

One of the most difficult challenges in my career came while building and sustaining high-performing teams. *Keeping them motivated* doesn't stop at that. It is about keeping them motivated consistently, especially during volatile, uncertain, complex, and ambiguous situations. Now, is motivation a newly evolved term? No. However, the term encompasses a broader and complex concept. Psychologically, motivation has a huge impact on a person's total well-being. It is something that conspires against all the lethargy, hopelessness, and fear and drives one to run towards the goal.

Motivation as a concept is easy to understand because every human has their own motivating elements. We all have at least a few experiences of how motivation drives us and probably have reaped the fruits of success as well.

The motivating factors are usually something of a reward or a benefit that one may obtain if one completes a certain task. Now, the reward is again a broad term. Each person carries a unique perspective about reward. To some, it is materialistic, whereas to others, it may be a word of approval or validation. It becomes crucial to evaluate the motivating factor to motivate your team in the right direction. And motivation remains the driving spirit of consistency.

The metrics used to assess and promote sustained performance are constantly evolving. What worked in the past may not suit the present or the future scenario. It has become critical to understand what to retain, where to apply a different approach, and what skills should be learned or unlearned. The ability to keep learning and to unlearn continuously would be an integral part of sustaining high-performing teams. There are some common components in any high-performing team; like, consistency in leadership, collaboration within the team, standing up for each other when the chips are down.

So, let's talk about the key components which sustain high-performing teams:

- We have to start with consistent clarity of direction. I have previously established how important it is to have a clear vision of where you want the team to lead. If there is no clarity of goal, you'll end up finding your team dispersed into multiple scenarios, doing loop-de-loops.
- The second component is the alignment of goals, with intent interdependence on each other. While setting the goal is a crucial step, it loses its significance if the individuals aren't aligned with the goals. The team must stay aligned towards the goal to attain success. It essentially helps them understand the priorities and abide by them. And the process can be smoothened further if employees at every level are communicated with the same.
- Building a culture of trust, collaboration, transparency, and accountability construe the third component.
- The recipe to building any good relationship is trust. If trust is initiated, everything else falls into place.
  It enables the team to collaborate, exchange feedback, and most importantly, to uplift and mentor each other, both as a team and in the individual space.

- Being supportive towards each other without any presumptions and partiality also plays a decent role towards high-performing teams. An indicator of a healthy relational infrastructure is the ability of the team members to communicate with each other openly. Development concerning high-performing teams is about dealing with the development of each member of the team to achieve the desired level of performance and productivity.
- I can't emphasize enough how important it is to keep building, refreshing, and developing high-performing teams to sustain them. It is highly necessary to acquire new skills while also retaining skills, still relevant. We must be sensible towards unlearning obsolete skills while learning newer ones.
- Infrastructure, development, support, encouragement, motivation, and financial and non-financial rewards; all act as enablers. These are the areas that must be addressed in order to maintain high-performing teams.
- Lastly, a long-term vision plays a critical part in retaining or sustaining high performing team. Short-term visions work momentarily, while a long-term vision helps people to work towards a bigger cause. And when we talk about short-term vision, it's very critical that we ensure that the vision is something that appeals to people, is relevant to organizations, serves as an inspiration, and also carries an element of stretch.

The Royal Society of London or the 'Invisible college' is an old and classic example of a high-performing team. Their motto happened to be *'Nullius in Verba'* which translates into, take nobody's word for it. The saying stood as an inspiration for all the members to verify the truths of the world with scientific facts and research. Sir Isaac Newton, Charles Darwin, Albert Einstein, and Stephen Hawking have all been a part of this society.

They included a wide variety of scientific branches like anatomy, astronomy, botany, chemistry, physics, and zoology. This society was able to produce so many important figures because they uplifted, supported, and gave each other constant feedback.

There was unsaid mentoring between each of them. The motivating factor was the individual spirit that inspired the other members to nourish the same within themselves.

They all sought inspiration from others' success and could grasp unintentional lessons. Through it all, they just stuck together to learn, unlearn, and relearn.

WHAT MAKES HIGH PERFORMING TEAM STICK TOGETHER?

Aligned goals, rewards, and consequences related to performance, a culture of collaboration, accountability, and continuous development, helping and keeping each other accountable make high-performing teams stick together. While we remain conscious of these elements, we must also remain aware of the factors that easily disintegrate a team.

"Conscious leadership is the intention, awareness, and choices designed to inform, impact and guide better thinking, feeling, and actions, to achieve meaningful and valuable results."— **Tony Dovale**. High-performing teams disintegrate loosely with a change in the leadership and more so if the leadership is not aligned to the previously set goals. Inconsistencies in leadership have proved to be the cause behind many inconvenient situations, along with comes a brutal process of change in human resources.

A new leader often brings in their own people and may not necessarily encourage people who have been working in the organization. A dearth of meritocracy culture often disintegrates high-performing teams. Similarly, disintegration often occurs while restructuring the organization during mergers and acquisitions, which come with a misalignment of culture and values.

The democratic leadership style is sometimes the core that keeps any team together. When every member's opinion, ideas, and voice is heard and respected, they feel valued and motivated. A great leader always instills a sense of purpose in his team members, which again binds them with the organization.

Disintegration may also occur due to a lack of focus on continued development or whenever stuck in the peculiar comfort zone. So often, we tend to get into a comfort zone and become aware of what works for us and end up feeling rather complacent. There's no substitute for consistent and continued hard work. We must challenge ourselves at regular intervals. As said before, consistency is the key to success and often comes in the form of a challenge.

Let me give an example of a team I was once leading.

It had performed admirably. In the past, they reached their level of incompetence to a point, which we refer to as **Peter Principle**. However, as soon as the team recognized the problem, they began reinventing, redeveloping, and realigning with the current environment and its goals and strategies. Soon they realized that their goals had to be realigned, and they had to focus on developing their own skills and learning a few new ones.

And over time, they could raise their bar. Being happy within the comfort zone and investing only in the past-tried skills often form a good reason for high-performing teams to disintegrate. We have to look at every job as a new challenge, every milestone to achieve as a new challenge. That keeps one energized and induces an urge to keep developing. It helps people to keep growing within the organization. Growth can either be vertical by doing bigger, broader jobs or horizontal by doing different types of jobs and acquiring new skills.

WHAT SHOULD YOU DO TO RETAIN HIGH-PERFORMING TEAMS?

- The first step to retaining or sustaining high-performing teams is to set clear goals. Ensure those goals are specific, measurable Build an attainable goal that may be strange but result-oriented and time-bound. Create a clear vision, an inspirational, relevant vision, and has an element of stretch.
- And, it should encompass the feeling of elation on achieving those visual inputs. One must maintain a focus on ongoing development.
- CPD, or Continuing Professional Development, is the continuous process of developing, maintaining, and documenting one's professional skills. These abilities can be acquired formally, through courses or training, or informally, on the job, or by observing others.
- Formal training can be provided by attending mentoring programs or by hiring external coaches. I've seen it work very well in sports teams and also in business teams. There have been fantastic results when we have a team coach working with the team continuously, much like the sports coach.

- They identify areas where the team is becoming complacent or requires new skills. So, I would recommend hiring a team coach who can help you become better and more consistent. Your next focus should be on development.
- Continue to benchmark yourself. Not only internally within your organization or with other teams, but also externally with the best in class. Let's understand this with an example.
- If you're running a 100-meter sprint or a marathon, your benchmark should be the current world record. But what if there isn't one. So, as stated in the title, you do not break or exceed the world record.
- That becomes your turning point. Once you set the record, you recall it. Savor it, and strive to beat it, and set a new world record. Benchmarking is critical in developing, sustaining, and retaining high-performing teams.

WHAT CAUSES THE HIGH PERFORMING TEAMS TO DISENGAGE?

The high-performing teams are disengaged due to a lack of clarity in goals, leadership changes, mergers and acquisitions, and a failure to align their performance, which neither translates into career growth nor awards. And in turn, they are not properly rewarded. I've also witnessed them disengage when they don't see immediate success. As a result, high-performing teams become disengaged when they are unable to achieve success over an extended period of time. You must lead people to success while keeping them motivated and ensuring that they do not give up. Instill resilience in the team. No team can win every game, but losing out on a few shouldn't bog you down. When they lose a match, they must come back stronger, better, and more powerful. And a team's leader, as well as key influencers, play a critical role in shaping up such a mentality. It is not always the manager or the leader who leads the team; members of the team often take on multiple leadership roles. Sometimes, members take up the role of an influencer and motivate others, while many a time, they do act as a mentor for each other. They could be a peer mentor or a friend. It could be a co-worker who constructively challenges or acts as an information gatherer.

Team members play a variety of roles based on their inherent strength.

CASE STUDY:

Let me now discuss a case study of a large technology company that has a global presence in seven countries.

This company had a 45-year of legacy and was a part of a conglomerate that contributed 25% of the conglomerate's mobile revenues to the world. As a result, as a part of the group's consolidation strategy, one of them is more profitable. The group desired to divest a portion of their business to obtain a high valuation. They were able to secure a good deal, paying nearly ten times the business's annual revenue.

They sold it, and the existing business or retained organization was left with only half of its revenue. They had a large cash reserve, which they obtained primarily from the proceeds of the sale of a profitable business division. The team had done well in the past, had controlled double-digit growth, and had, in fact, grown above the organization's rate of growth. They had grown largely due to their ability to drive operational excellence and their ability to retain existing customers by consistently providing high-quality, cost-effective service delivery. But with divesting one of their key operating arms, they had to rethink their strategy and focus on a new line of growth considering the post-pandemic situation.

In this transition phase, they're moving into a very traditional business process-oriented management company driven mostly by operational excellence parameters. They had to now focus on driving business on a new line of s digital growth. Thus, they had to reinvent their strategy, like how digitization was going to contribute and how they are planning to grow digital, organic, or inorganic. That is how the digital was a fraction focusing on how digital only contributed to 5% of current revenues? How can we increase the digital wallet's digital share to more than 60%? And, what kind of structure would they require? One's strategy is also centered on the types of businesses one wishes to acquire. How would one like to strengthen one's internal capabilities? How does one see through the transition? As per the existing challenges, the organization was now creating a clear strategy defining what it does with the existing BPM business and how one grows the digital business. In this case, it took a long time to conclude a proper strategy. There was a vision; they liked to return to the same size and transform from the button size of 300 million USD to 1 billion USD in five years.

That was almost 4x growth in five years. However, even with a great rate of customer retention of about 95 percent, they could not acquire new customers. Significantly, the company has grown due to selling and upselling. Their rate of growth was indeed better than the industrial rate. Nevertheless, as it was mainly through upselling and cross-selling, they did not have much of the market insights.

Top it all; they had to create a clear structure with two different verticals, namely, the BPM business and the digital business. BPM is an abbreviation for Business Process Management. It is a technological solution that automates organizational business processes. As a result, businesses have more opportunities and increased efficiency while putting in less effort and spending less money.

Furthermore, BPM facilitates the organization to have control of all the work processes. In comparison, digital business is the one that leverages technology in both internal and external operations. Since the Internet became widely available to businesses and individuals, information technology has changed the infrastructure and operation of businesses. They examined the BPM business and restructured it, which was once managed by the existing leadership team.

However, for the digital business, the organization had to bring in a new leader from the outside with prior experience in growing businesses both organically and inorganically. Thus, the leader was now an outsider.

They invested a significant portion of the proceeds from the acquisition and leveraged it to deploy it in their business. And in the BPM industry, it was more about achieving incremental growth through consolidation, the addition of new customers, and investment in technology to make the process more efficient.

Additionally, investing in data analytics helped in the establishment of the Centre of Excellence. They diversified their efforts to the other digital business-like, software solutions, consulting practice, and analytics. The organizational structure was now restructured into two distinct verticals. They were now able to segment the sales team into a specialized group, thus designing a sales organization structure. The regions you serve, the number of products and services you offer, the size of your sales team, and the size and industry of your customers will all influence how you organize your sales team. One was dedicated to the BPM business for sales and customer relationship management, which was not done previously.

Thus, the sales organization was now divided into two parts: one for the BPM business and another for the digital business. The sales organization had one team that was looking at the business growth that is, acquiring new customers. And another team was dedicated to customer relationship management. Earlier, you had one sales team selling both products and managing the customer relations. There was a lack of clarity and focus in the sales team with not much focus on the digital business. Now the team was structured as per the business verticals as separate P&Ls. Two separate teams that had a separate sales organization and the right kind of impact was created, which then drove the right culture. Instead of designing a culture primarily on operational efficiency, we're now intended to look at a culture based on innovation and a consultative selling and consultative approach while providing solutions.

Let us understand the two approaches. Innovation culture functions as a type of cross-cutting culture, with all process participants shaping and supporting its standards and values. A positive innovation culture provides incentives to the employees and leads to an increase in the company's innovative strength. Rather than selling a product or service, consultative selling focuses on the customer's needs and experiences.

Consultative selling is a sales approach that emphasizes relationships and open dialogue to identify and address a customer's needs. It is more concerned towards the customer than with the product being sold. All of this, in turn, necessitated a significant shift in the mindset. So, it began with hiring the right people from outside sources, followed by extensive culture-building workshops or innovation labs that encouraged people to think differently. The organization invested in Culture and Innovation Labs, and it was applied to everyone in the organization, which had close to 30,000 full-time equivalents, or FTEs.

As a result, it was branded as an innovation and customer-first program. It helped to create and communicate what culture the organization wanted to go forward to. There was then a translation, clear strategic goals that were aligned with the leadership, key result areas, and key performance indicators. The balanced scorecard method was used to implement the same. The balanced scorecard is a strategic planning methodology that corporate executives use to balance financial (stockholder) concerns, customer concerns, and operational process and innovation concerns in their day-to-day operations.

The balanced scorecard is built on four pillars: financial, business process, customer, and organizational capacity. It enables organizations to identify their flaws and devise strategies to overcome them. This was then translated down the line to individual contributors. With all the aforementioned attributes added, the organization was able to stay focused on its core objective. Despite the impact of the pandemic, it had shown a record profit in the first year itself, and it certainly appears to be on the path to success.

TAKEAWAYS:

- **Reinvent yourself.** Whether the business goes through restructuring, realignment, merger, or acquisition, and even if everything happens at the same time, in a pandemic situation like this, you must be prepared to realign. Always be flexible, be agile, and be adaptable to the new changes in the environment.
- **Have a well-defined strategy and vision in place.** Having an ambiguous vision adds a layer of complication. Indeed, one of the challenges for the organization is keeping people motivated, particularly during mergers and acquisitions.

The following ways can help to boost employee engagement during mergers and acquisitions:

- **Let your values guide your actions.** Ensure that all integration and synergy-related decisions, actions, and communications are consistent with the culture and underlying values. Always keep in mind that current, new, or departing employees, as well as your customers and investors, are constantly watching the company's behavior.
- **Over-communicate.** During a merger, executives should enhance their communication game by holding town hall-style meetings and encouraging managers to meet one-on-one with their teams to answer questions.

  They must legally communicate both good and bad news as soon as possible. Employees want to know the truth, and the sooner they do, the better they can mentally and practically prepare for their future.
- **Empathize.** Mergers or acquisitions are tumultuous.

Many executives forget to empathize while focusing on the bigger picture. HR managers must assist leaders in focusing on the company and the people who make it run, and they must encourage them to express their genuine appreciation and concern for employees' well-being. Even in the most difficult of times, an empathetic leader can galvanize the workforce.

Coaching and outplacement services and an open-door policy for managers whose teams have questions should be available to their leaders.

- **Engaging with those who are leaving.** Managers may begin to ignore employees who are about to be laid off, but these workers are critical to a smooth transition. If they are not assisted, they can demoralize the whole working ambiance and can even harm the company's name on social media platforms.

  Employees who are not being laid off do pay close attention to how you treat the employees. Their decision to stay or leave the organization is influenced by the change they see in your attitude. If you treat departing employees with kindness and respect and assist them in finding new employment, they will do a better job and help spread a positive atmosphere throughout the company.

- **Involve employees in the transition.** Companies include dozens of committees, task forces, and teams to help with the transition during a merger or acquisition. HR should explain the benefits of serving on them and recruit high-performing individuals to participate. Being a part of a transition team allows employees to hone their project management and analytical skills. And there is no better way to learn about collaboration than to bring people from two different corporate cultures together to work towards a common goal. Employee engagement faces significant challenges as a result of mergers and acquisitions. Companies, on the other hand, can go a long way while keeping workers motivated and productive, both during the transition and also during the critical first weeks of launching the new organization. Communicating honestly and frequently, expressing empathy, and involving employees in important decisions are some of the key steps to involve the employees during the transition process.

People are concerned about whether they have a job or not. Keeping them motivated requires a clear strategy, a clear vision, the right structure to support that vision, the right culture to drive it forward, and also the right people in the right roles, even if it requires a restructuring of the organization.

- If the organization is forced to let go and offer a voluntary payment scheme to some leadership team members who were unable to handle the situation or lacked the required skills, or harbored the mindset of leaving the organization in the future, the following points must be emphasized right away.
- It is also about equipping the organization with the necessary skills and effectively communicating the vision to every team member, right from the organization's head, the CEO of the business, to the individual contributors on the job, which can be accomplished through a series of workshops.
- Finally, it is a matter of translating our tables' key performance indicators and business codes into performance and rewards.

So, knowing what behaviors to expect, what goals to strive for, the rewards and consequences of achieving or failing to achieve those goals ensure that the teams are driven to high standards of performance.

8

ENGAGING AND MOTIVATING HIGH PERFORMING TEAMS.

"If you are not willing to risk the usual, you will have to settle for the ordinary."
-Jim Rohn

Willing to take a risk is the first sign of thinking out of the box. Basking in the comfort zone can give us pleasure; however, it can never make us stand apart. It is the 21st century, and human resource is the essential ingredient of an organization. No matter how far we develop technology, nothing can replace the human mind's capacity, which is always driven to excel further.

Right from childhood, we dream of becoming something, which is often reflected in the games we play. Have we not played a role of shopkeeper or teacher or a doctor? Yes, we did. In fact, half of our childhood is spent answering people about our ambitions. Now, as you read this book as the professional you always wanted to become, you do realize that the path to achieving your dreams was never easy.

Hurdles form the most crucial part of our journey. There were times when we all have thought of giving up. We lacked the motivational drive.

We failed to find the purpose. There comes a situation when we want to perform but do not. Why? The answer to this question lies in motivation. As soon as we get motivated to do something great, something extraordinary, we withstand the hurdles.

We practice. We perform. We achieve our goals.

Before I begin to highlight the significance of engaging and motivating high-performing teams, I must remind my readers that business environments are nothing less than a battlefield. And be it business or a battle, no one can win by having the best of men or the best of technology, processes. One can win only by ensuring that one has the best people working who are engaged and motivated towards the goal. Keeping the teams engaged and motivated consistently is a key to successfully creating high-performing teams where the high-performance index is sustained. These statements may sound overused.Nevertheless, understanding the essence and the spirit of these words shall determine the strategy of ensuring that a person is able to sustain a high-performing team.

I am often asked the real meaning of engaging and motivating people. Simply put, it means that people are excited to do their job; they are placed in a suitable working ambiance with the right energy where they are willing to perform to their full potential. Now, there are various ways to keep employees motivated and engaged, whether through financial benefits or non-financial modes. The financial model of motivation comes via the pay packages. No organization is asked to overpay to retain an employee. However, every organization must follow market standards. Paying the deserved package at an appropriate time is crucial.

Let me give an example. A doctorate degree holder must be hired for a scientific position and not for a role of a technical assistant. If we analyze the statistics of the global attrition rate, we shall understand how improper pay scale contributes to the increasing rate of attrition. On the same note, I would also highlight the significance of a conducive working environment. There have been cases when highly qualified individuals left a high-paying job and opted for a 60% pay-cut.

Money is not everything. An individual can be allured to an organization through an affluent pay package; however, there are other variables that influence their decision to leave. Companies look at rewarding compensation financially in various ways. By giving them a niche pay allowance for skills that are hard to acquire from the market or hard to develop.

This is typically used in the technology industry. People have a special allowance called a niche skill allowance which is given for certain critical technical skills that are not easily available in the market. Different organizations follow different rules while paying the niche pay allowance. It is either given as a yearly allowance or as a long-term incentive plan to be paid every three years. Or the lump sum can be broken down to 30% for the first two years and then 40% for the third year.

Employee stock option is another way of rewarding performance.

The technology firms have been the pioneers in starting the employee stock options; however, this policy is now extended to FMCG, pharmaceuticals, and manufacturing firms who are now proactive in rewarding their employees. Very recently, we have seen a large steel organization that has extended stock options, right from the top management to the senior management, junior management, and middle management, and even to the blue-collar employees. They have given them stock options with the company.

I have a curious experience as HR in a public listed company. The conventional norm was to incentivize only the senior management, but then the scheme was extended to individual contributors who were a part of the company payroll. This, in turn, created a high level of performance as the employees developed a sense of ownership and commitment towards their tasks as well as towards the organizational goal. And, as they say, when people feel ownership towards any entity, they tend to be more dedicated to bringing success to the organization. Variable pay and bonus contribute to another aspect of financial rewards.

These days, organizations are more focused on adding variable pay than fixed pay. In the higher incentive packages, one can find more variable pays than fixed pays. This global shift of paying mindset ensures that every employee gets paid for the basic cost of living and achieves an additional delta. So, where does the difference lie? Even the fixed pay is paid to take care of the living expenses as per the cost of living in that particular country or city. Variable pay is a clearer measure of performance.

One must maintain the said standard of performance to receive the benefits of variable pay. The better the individual performs, the higher would be their incentive. Incentives or bonuses are key motivators for better performance. While fixed pay is given to get the job done, incentives declare an employee's better performance.

That is why variable pay plays a very important role in driving performance. Monetary compensation brings along recognition for the employee's performance. The associated recognition designs the factors that influence variable pay. In a consulting business, the consultant is paid annually or quarterly or paid on a project-to-project basis. This is entirely dependent on the business model, the cash flow situation of the organization, and the seasonality of the business. In one of my surveys, I have found that 35% of the business leaders and HR heads recognize the variable pay to go a long way in incentivizing performance. More than 35% have contributed to an important measure of retaining high-performing teams.

Let us now analyze the non-financial ways of rewarding performance. Let me tell you that the non-financial mode has its own charm for motivating the employees.

Awards:
- Here, I am not pointing at any cash prize. If you are familiar with professional social media platforms like LinkedIn, you have certainly come across employers posting about their star employees. This is more like a token of appreciation. If an organization aims to retain high-performers, it must provide appreciation and recognition openly.
- Star employee of the quarter and star employee of the year are some non-financial ways to motivate the employees to perform better. One can even notice such appreciation of the employees in an organization's website too.

Promotions:
- A rise in the status and responsibilities make the employee feel trusted. When an organization entrusts an employee with bigger responsibilities, the employee is motivated to excel.
- Job enrichment programs have brought in a gust of fresh air to the job specificities. Job enrichment refers to advancing or moderating the tasks to impart more freedom, flexibility, and growth for the employee.

Job security:
- An assurance of a job is more like a constant flow of income for the employees.

- Apart from the work culture, pay scale, a sense of job security helps in the retention of the employees.

Motivation and engagement go hand in hand. Both must coexist in a symbiotic relationship in any organizational model. Engagement comprises a series of tasks that induce motivation among the employees. It is not a herculean task to create engaging activities within an organization. Some are listed below:

Recreational activities: This can be as simple as playing cards or board games. It is bound to bring a spirit of fun. A moment of freedom from routine work allows the employees to bond with each other and connect beyond the workspace. An annual trip or a rendezvous event can introduce a dramatic change in the way employees come together.

Workshops: Conducting workshops include the element of collaboration and participation. Organizational psychology has proven that learning is enhanced when a friendly colleague is teaching. Top it all, collaboration often kindles new ideas and thus helps in the team's overall growth.

Career progression: In my own career, I have noticed that a lot of people want to stay in organizations where they find a scope of progress in the provided job profile. A high-performing team desires both vertical and horizontal progression. A team that is bestowed with a clear vision, measurable targets to achieve, along with the right kind of appreciation and rewards, the retention rate is more pronounced.

Coaching and Mentoring: Every high-performing team is driven by results. They are dedicated to acquiring advanced skills, whether technical or functional or leadership skills. The organization must identify the plausible qualities within the individuals and train them appropriately. The performance of the team is enhanced when each member is contributing with one's unique talent. Honing the inherent talent through timely mentoring engages a high-performing team. At various levels, technical and functional training in the individual contributor level or the first-time manager level could be in the range of 50 to 70% of the training. In technical and functional training, a substantial amount of time, effort, and budget must be invested. For first-time managers, at least 30% of the budget should be spent.

One can say 30 to 50% of budgets should be dedicated towards leadership training. However, for mid-level and senior executives, more than 50% of the budget should be spent on leadership training.

A range of 50-70% of the development budget should be allocated for executive coaching. As I conducted a survey across the business heads, CEOs, CHROs, and learning and development heads, I arrived at a conclusion that 80% of the aforementioned were providing the right kind of training at the right time. This, in turn, served as the single largest factor for retaining, sustaining, and motivating high-performing teams.

Career paths: A career is free to progress vertically as well as horizontally. The career path is designed based on the employee's knowledge, skills, certifications, and experience. With the right kind of coaching and mentoring, a high-performing employee can decide on his/her career progression. If an organization is able to provide appropriate upgradation of skills at the right time, the high-performing team shall stick to the organization.

There is a famous quote by American Novelist Alice Walker. *"The most common way people give up their power is by thinking they don't have any."* This quote is appropriate while an organization creates a high-performing team. Every employee carries an inherent skill, and it is the organization's duty to mold that skill for the benefit of the organization. Individual goals must be inclined with the organizational mission.

On the same note, the employee must be provided with constant feedback to make them realize where they stand in the bigger picture.

"The tragedy of life does not lie in not reaching your goal. The tragedy lies in having no goals to reach."
– Dr. Benjamin E. Mays

As we proceed to discern the sequential approach to performance management, let me ask you to think about your last performance review. Don't we often sit down pondering on what went wrong and what went right? The very first kind of review we receive in life is through our progress report card in the school.

A progress report card measures the amount of knowledge a student has gained from the lessons taught in the class. Students sit for a test, and their performance is graded. However, the scenario at the job is different.

It is more application-oriented. The effective application of the gained knowledge for the cumulative success of the organization determines an employee's performance.

There are various factors involved to assess the performance. How efficient and effective is an employee towards achieving the organizational goal? If you are wondering about the difference in efficiency and effectivity, let me summarize both in the simplest terms. Efficiency is about speed, while effectivity is about the quality of the outcome.

The second factor revolves around the extent of supervision and guidance the employee needs. A self-starter employee is the first requisite of a high-performing team.

During my training sessions, I often ask: What kind of thought comes to your mind when you see your performance report? You will be surprised to know that 80% of the participants declare it as not a great experience.

In fact, a lot of employees leave the organization after their performance appraisal. Many HR practitioners have disclosed that performance reviews lead to attrition.

The reason behind attrition often includes the following:

- Rating standards are not clearly communicated. Review and feedback are neither timely nor consistent.
- The organization often lacks the right kind of infrastructure for timely coaching and mentoring.
- Expectations from the employees are not clearly demarcated.
- Statistically, 80% of the global workforce is dissatisfied with their job profile.

If employees are shown the bigger picture, they turn more enthusiastic towards performing. As mentioned earlier, merging the individual's goal with the organizational goal impacts team performance and organizational growth.

Secondly, as the employees fetch benefits, both financially and non-financially, they improve their performance and prefer to remain with the same organization.

The steps to develop an engaging and high-performing team are sequential. One leads to another, and if the organization loses one aspect in the process, the motivation amongst the employees is lost.

Thus, once a high-performing team loses its efficacy.

TAKEAWAYS:

- Consider both financial and non-financial rewards while introducing the system of rewards and recognition for performance appraisal.
- Pay-scale incentives should follow the market standard. An organization's incentive policy must drive the employees to perform well.
- Investing in the learning and development of the employees enhances the chance of employee retention.
- A high-performing team with proper motivation and engagement can be retained with consistent performance.

9

INTEGRATED PERFORMANCE MANAGEMENT IN DRIVING HIGH-PERFORMING TEAMS

"Performance should be an expectation of employment, and it is the leaders' job to create an environment where maximum performance is possible."

– Rob Burn

Every employee, regardless of the position or level in the organization, is hundred percent accountable for their own career growth. While we have analyzed the various factors that influence the making of a high-performing team, there exist various strategies of performance management that drive the consistent growth of high-performing teams.

Developing skills is just one aspect of nurturing high-performing teams. A good HR system of an organization can apply different methods to hone the inherent managerial skills of its employees and improve overall performance.

However, the challenge remains in monitoring the performance. Without constant monitoring of the performance chart, it is impossible to retain the high-performing teams. Consistent tracking of performance opens the room for the required modification and improvisation. It provides a complete assessment of how the team is performing reacting towards the training and development process.

An accurate assessment helps in developing the correct tools for improving the performance; however, a wrong assessment may drown even the best-performing team. A systematic process of planning, managing, measuring, reviewing, rewarding, and improving the performance of an individual employee or a team, or an organization is called Performance Management. (Put the performance management picture here, which is there in the ppt.)

The key objectives of the performance management system are as follows:

- Provide an accurate classification of performance expectations by highlighting the key result areas. The employees must be motivated to convert the KRAs (Key Result Areas) into KPIs (Key Performance Indicators)
- Apply the SMART analogy for identifying the KRAs. They should be Specific, Measurable, Attainable, Relevant, and Time-bound (SMART)
- Set the performance standard and the parameters to measure the performance. The parameters should be unbiased.
- The employee/team must be clear with the team's or organization's objective. Conflicting ideologies are not conducive for high-performing teams.
- The relationship between the team members and also with the leader should be open, and communication should be free. A true leader always encourages the employees. The leader must lead towards better performance by honing the skills of every team member.
- Strengthen relationships and communication. It is about ensuring that people understand the right criteria for measuring their performance. They will also get an opportunity to clarify how they are going to achieve those deliverables.
- Identify the technical, functional, behavioral, and organizational loopholes to bridge the performance gaps.
- Identify the training and development needs for improving the overall performance of an organization and invest in the required infrastructure.
- Assess the performance accurately and provide feedback to improvise.

- Reward and recognition are an integral part of the performance management system.
- Promote performance culture in the organization. Employees must be drawn to perform well.

The process of evaluating performance varies from one organization to another. However, the ground rules remain the same. The sequence of evaluation is more or less similar in all kinds of organizations. Here is the step-by-step demonstration of performance evaluation:

Self-Assessment: The first step of performance assessment begins at the individual level. The employee evaluates how they have performed against the set targets. The best plausible way to do self-assessment is by analyzing each key result area, the significant achievements, and challenges you have faced while achieving the target. As you do the objective assessment, you follow the rating scale to arrive at what is expected of you and how far you stand from the expectations. On the same note, one has to understand that every performance cannot fall under the category of outstanding performance. Consistent performance means touching the mark of expected performance.

Immediate Manager's Assessment: Once the self-assessment is completed, the performance is assessed by the immediate managers. Even in that case, performance should be assessed considering one key result at a time. A manager must not start with an overall assessment. Every key result area is assigned with a specific weightage.

A manager has to rate the performance as per the weightage assigned and then proceed to an overall assessment of performance. The manager must provide qualitative feedback to the employee, emphasizing the points to work upon for better performance. If need be, identify the training needs.

Skip level Manager Assessment: The rating of the immediate manager is then validated by the skip-level managers. Some organizations have committees to assess the rating provided by the immediate managers to analyze the performance of an employee.

Decide on the Reward System: Once the rating is provided, the senior managers decide on the rewarding system.

The rewards and recognition can be project-based or quarterly, or annually. The previous chapter has a detailed breakdown of the various reward system.

WHAT IS THE PERFORMANCE MANAGEMENT CYCLE?

One of the most crucial parts of the performance management process is the performance management cycle. It is a four-step procedure of planning, monitoring, reviewing, and rewarding. An organization follows these four steps to increasing its structural flexibility, employee motivation, and competency in the market. As stated, the cycle has four stages,

1. Planning
2. Monitoring
3. Reviewing
4. Rewarding

This traditionally run model ends with a performance review at the end of the year. However, these days, many organizations have found that even average employees can turn into high-performing teams with more frequent check-in of performance. The main aim of the performance management cycle is to provide the employee with proper guidelines or a roadmap to reach the company's objectives. Let's have a detailed look at the various stages one by one.

Planning: This is the stepping stone of conceiving success. Before an employee is entitled to a particular job, the management team decides on the organizational objectives of the year. This includes the overall strategy for the business, including the developmental goals, specific targets, actions, and behaviors. Once the management team chalks out the plan, it is time to include the employee in the strategic planning of the year. As I have said earlier, it is a collaborative process. None can stay singular.

Planning must lead to the development of SMART goals.

Specific- The management must cross-check if the goal is clearly outlined and detailed information is provided to the employees to achieve. So, is your objective precise before you indulge it to the employees?

Measurable- This is a tricky part. The goal must have a measurable indicator to tell if it has been achieved.

Now, how does one identify and define what good performance is and what isn't?

Attainable- The goal must stretch the employee but never to an unrealistic level. A stretch of 20 to 30% is acceptable. However, anything that can be achieved easily doesn't qualify.

Relevant- The organization must ensure that the said goal is in line with the employee's job profile and overall goals of the organization. As they say, a fish's capabilities cannot be judged by its ability to fly. Can we? Any objective should be relevant.

Time-bound- There should be a definite timeline to finish a task. But again, it cannot be unrealistic. Based on the HR guidelines of an organization, the monthly, quarterly, or yearly goals are set for the employees.

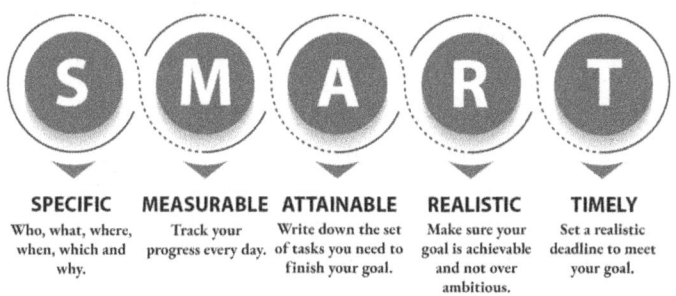

SPECIFIC	MEASURABLE	ATTAINABLE	REALISTIC	TIMELY
Who, what, where, when, which and why.	Track your progress every day.	Write down the set of tasks you need to finish your goal.	Make sure your goal is achievable and not over ambitious.	Set a realistic deadline to meet your goal.

During this stage of planning, the management identifies the key areas where the employees need training and development. Once the management shows a keen interest in the employee development plan, the employees get motivated as they see the management assisting them in building a high-performance team. Once the goals are set, they must be communicated effectively. There have been many scenarios where the management does not communicate the goals effectively, which in turn results in the collapse of this cycle before even it begins.

Without translating your vision into an inspiring idea to the employees, without motivating them to work for it, the performance management cycle cannot begin.

As the respected thought leader Sybil F. Stershic quotes,
*"The way your **employees** feel is the way your customers will feel. And if your **employees** don't feel valued, neither will your customers."*

Monitoring: In the performance management cycle, monitoring is the key to checking the achievements. However, in this fast-paced organizational growth and increasing competition, monitoring will not be effective if done only once a year. As I experienced, good management meets the employees on a monthly and quarterly basis, not only to assess the extent of task completed but also to offer help in solving any problems, adjust target, if needed. As we see, organizational goals are bound to be long-term. They cannot plan on day-to-day basis. However, too large and far-off goals are intimidating. Making monthly sub-goals often smoothens the process. Goals can shift during a year considering the economic and political scenario. Frequent meetings allow the introduction of new or modified goals.

Monitoring of goals helps one predict future growth as well. One can anticipate the external and internal factors that may affect the performance and make sure those obstacles are dealt with.

Reviewing: One can see it as an opportunity to collaborate with the employees in a better way. The more the employees are included in the performance management cycle, the more they will be motivated to work diligently towards the set target. With proper monitoring, management would already have a fair idea about the performance of the employees during the year.

Reviewing helps in evaluating the final result and the process as well. Reviews can be informal or formal. Informal reviews play an important role because they give timely feedback. One can do it weekly, fortnightly, monthly, or every quarter.

I recommend a monthly review of the key result areas. However, if people are working on a project, I recommend a weekly review or a review every fortnight. While the formal reviews happen once in six months or once a year, it definitely serves a very important purpose. It gives the right kind of weightage on rewards.

Sometimes, instead of course correction, it becomes more of a post-mortem. Doing it earlier can, in fact, gives the employee an opportunity to correct the performance graph well in advance.

The review takes place only to enable the right feedback. A timely, constructive criticism is the essence of employee motivation and retention. While giving the feedback, I recommend a quick evaluation.

The management must ask a few questions. Was the original goal realistic? Did the employee gain any experience or skills? Did the organization provide ample support to the employee for the completion of the task? If you get yes for the above questions, then you must assess what is holding the employee back, why the employee is not able to perform. Analyzing these questions may help the management comprehend the external and internal factors that influence the performance. The second significant part is documenting the review process/feedback. Corporates often undergo changes in the managerial levels and an employee's past performance must be documented and saved.

This ensures that the employees do not lose out on their scorecard even if the boss is new. Employees' functional skills, interpersonal skills, communication skills, technical skills, everything must be documented. Documentation, in turn, helps to discern the training requirements.

Rewarding: It is a stage that can never be overlooked. Employees, if they do not get rewarded after striving towards the organizational goal for a year, they lose faith in the organization. Whether an organization gives financial or non-financial rewards, it doesn't matter as long as a rewarding system prevails in the organization.

PEOPLE EXCELLENCE THROUGH ACHIEVEMENT AND KNOWLEDGE (PEAK):

It is a cohesive approach to the performance management system that results in improvement of organizational effectiveness and capabilities, organizational sustainability and enhances both organizational and personal learning. There are several contributors to PEAK.

- Type of leadership
- Management and development of knowledge
- Strategic Planning of the goal
- Focus on the employee needs
- Operational focus
- Importance of results

An integrated strategy of progressive innovation and continuous improvement helps in achieving high-performing teams.

Innovation is quite convoluted. It can be easily identified but difficult to apply and manage. Bridging the knowledge gap by improvising on the techniques plays a key role in promoting high-performing culture. PEAK refers to

- Holistic Performance Management System
- Tool for Employee Development
- Tool for Promoting a Culture for High Performance

While developing a holistic approach to analyzing performance, there are some common mistakes that leaders often commit to avoid any conflicting consequences.

Halo/Horns Effect: The tendency of a manager to rate the employee the same in every trait. It is like carrying a preconceived notion. Either an employee is good at everything, or the employee is bad at everything. The right way of performance rating is not judging the personality but the performance.

Central Tendency: To avoid conflict or controversy amongst the employees, managers tend to rate every employee the same. They avoid differentiation.

Leniency: Another way to avoid conflict in the workspace is by showing leniency. Managers do not provide honest reviews, rather remain lenient while rating.

Recency: An employee's performance cannot be rated by focusing on narrow objectives. Performance must be assessed for an entire year and not for one particular project.

Constancy: Rating an employee for the present year by seeing their previous year's records is not a good sign of a performance management system.

WHAT IS PERFORMANCE EQUATION?

Performance equation is about defining performance in a quantitative manner. As we understand, performance is about how easily, effectively, and quickly employees achieve the set target.

To define it quantitatively, one needs to incorporate a few factors.

Performance = KPI score + Competency/ Behaviors

What does performance equate to?

Key Aspects of Performance Management:
- KRAs- List of responsibilities for a job
- KPIs – List of means of achieving KRAs
- Measures of success – Benchmarks for evaluating performance
- Weightage – To stress the importance of the elements in assessing the total performance. Everything need not be given the same weightage. It can be split between different KRAs.

BUILDING A PERFORMANCE SCORE CARD

While building the performance scorecard, every KRA is assigned a specific weightage. Similarly, every KRA has a specific KPI, i.e., the modes to achieve the KRAs.

The following table can give a clearer view of how a performance scorecard is maintained.

KRA	KPI	KPI Weightage
Increase Average Revenue (50%)	Increase 30% revenue from existing customers in 6 months	30%
	Additional 20% revenue from new customers in 6 months	20%
Sales Development (20%)	Achieve individual sales target of Rs. 10,00,000	10%
	Achieve team target of Rs. 30,00,000	10%
Customer Acquisition (20%)	To ensure that we get at least 20 new clients for the financial year	10%
	The break up of 20 new clients should be : 60% agency business & 40% Direct clients	10%
Maintain Quality (10%)	Maintain average bug density/defect density per assignment. Total number bugs should not exceed 10 per code file during code reviews.	10%
Total Weightage = 100%		100%

COMPETENCY IN PERFORMANCE MANAGEMENT

In management terms, competencies are a cluster of behaviors that are measurable and observable. One can see if an employee is keen on performing, enthusiastic towards the organizational goal. Competency, when demonstrated by employees, results in success. Studying competency occurs at a different stage of employment right from the recruitment process. The KRAs for an employee is often decided based on the inherent competencies of the employee.

In alignment with The People Way, all employees (Non-CFS) are rated on the following competencies/ behavior.

- **Solving problems:** The competency of solving problems includes the ability to solve problems through multiple criteria. The employee must identify and assess the plausible responses towards the problem. They should possess a variety of problem-solving and analytical approaches to address the challenge and also the ability to evaluate alternative courses of action.
  An employee who is competent in problem-solving attends to the root cause and not just the symptoms. Problem-solving competency brings a solution to conflicting constraints.
- **Influencing people:** In a high-performing team, employees have to influence each other. New and difficult challenges open rooms of opportunities. Competency in influencing others is a crucial skill to gain the support, trust, or commitment of others.
- The ability to get people to change their attitude, behavior, and mindset and direct them towards the organizational target is one of the key competencies needed in a high-performing team.
  Good negotiation skills and effective listening helps in influencing people. On the same note, we must acknowledge the difference between persuasion and manipulation. Manipulating employees by showing lucrative offers ultimately demotivates the employees and paves the path towards attrition.
- **Ability to adapt:** Another key competency for a high-performing team is the ability to adapt to the changing nature of the work, organizational goals, and technical advancements, and so on.
- **Delivering results:** Employees competent in delivering results on time form an integral part of a high-performing team.

- Here, we must acknowledge that the delivered result should be viable enough to consider the employee competent.
- Half-baked results do not contribute to the performance scorecard.

CASE STUDY:

Let's look at this case of a large multinational corporation, which was facing several issues while delivering peak performance.

It was a technology and business process outsourcing firm catering to global stakeholders in the communication space. Despite having a very strong brand name, they were not able to perform the audit to get the expected kind of performance. The reason was, there was no definitive strategy to deliver a key outcome or add value to the clients. The core strategy was focused on the products and lines of business, emerging markets as well as developed markets. The company had to look upon certain other factors like; what are the key differentiators? And who are the key stakeholders, and the level of engagement and support required for stakeholders? Then, what was the key messaging and communication? The answer to all is an adaptive strategy. The second crucial part is the right kind of organizational structure, the kind of leaders one should have. A lot of assigned leaders were from the telecom sector or from the parent company who hardly understood technology or the business process outsourcing industry. Thus, the working ambiance was disruptive, and the company was running more like a telecommunication company rather than a technology or business process outsourcing company.

The thought process was old, rigid, and followed the hierarchical model. Another challenge was the political interference from the parent company. They were more inclined towards their personal agendas, creating their personal empire rather than doing the right things for the business. The outcome was a toxic working environment. Hence, instead of focusing on doing what is right for the business and getting people from the right background who understand the business process industry and the technology industry and getting them to run the business. The business was more in a command-and-control style, and the recruitment or assignment was in a political style of planting the favorites of the parent company. They assigned people who are aligned to the parent company rather than people who are skilled and capable of doing the job and driving the business. In turn, the business developed a negative image in the external market. No good talent was attracted to this company anymore.

Moreover, a lot of people who were assigned by the parent company to the global technology sector were unfit to continue in the parent company and were almost on the verge of retirement. They used this as a parking lot.

The organization had to take a few major corrective steps.

- Appoint a new CEO who had a fair understanding of shared services and limited services.
- Hiring the head of HR from a similar background.
- Investing in the right organization with appropriate organizational strategy.
- Getting the right people with a technology background or a better business process background, hiring diverse talent from diverse companies.
- Looking at stakeholder engagement, stakeholder communication, cost-benefit analysis, differentiating production from what's available externally

By hiring the right people, investing a lot of efforts in employer branding, making the policies and HR processes, introducing the best class practices, investing in leadership development, line manager development, and a blended approach of technical and functional skills, the organization was recognized for good people practices within three years. It could attract and retain the right kind of talent and could keep them engaged.

By introducing employee motivation through financial and non-financial rewards, including an escape allowance, helped in retaining talent to a great extent. The dropout ratios, which were above the industry standards, reduced significantly.

As we go through the performance management system, we now know that high-performing teams are not made out of thin air. There prevails a need for intervention in terms of monitoring performance, providing timely feedback, timely training, and development for improving individual skills, motivating to be consistent in performance, and finally rewarding for achieving the performance.

The whole cycle of the performance management system plays the most essential role in making a high-performing team.

To conclude, let me quote Leonardo Da Vinci here,

"Knowing is not enough; we must apply. Willing is not enough; we must do it."

TAKEAWAYS:

- Good performance management helps the team align to the goals and objectives of the organization while improving their skills.
- It begins with the proper planning of goals.
- With clarity in goals, performance takes off well.
- Goals should be conveyed to the entirety of your staff in such a way that they understand and are motivated to work towards it.
- Once the goal is understood, performance can be monitored.
- Timely feedback must follow the monitoring process. Feedback opens the door for training and development. Rigorously following this allows one to boost their performance in the areas required.
- Once there is a considerable improvement in the required areas, individuals should be compensated for their efforts in terms of financial or non-financial rewards.

10

DEVELOPING YOUR LEADERSHIP CAPABILITY IN LEADING AND INSPIRING OTHERS

"Good managers are not necessarily good leaders, but great leaders make outstanding managers."

Leadership is something that is often misrepresented and inaptly defined in English. The bookish definition defines leadership as a process by which a manager or executive guides, directs, and influences the behaviors of others towards the completion of a goal. We can consider leadership as a quality of the managers to induce the subordinates to work towards the organizational goal with confidence and enthusiasm.

My perspectives see leadership as a journey of continuous reflection and improvisation. It is an opportunity for one to raise one's own bar of performance, inspire others to improve their performances, and achieve their maximum potential.

The responsibility attached to a leader's position is huge. As Keith Davis once quoted,

"It is the human factor which binds a group together and motivates it towards its goal."

We have to understand here that not all managers become good leaders; however, a great leader is always an outstanding manager. Turn the pages of history, and you will be bestowed with a list of great leaders. Remember Princess Diana shaking hands with an AIDS patient? There, she showed the power of compassion and tried to convey the message that AIDS doesn't transmit through touch. We have global leaders like Malala Yusuf fighting for women's rights and leading the populace towards the power of resilience. And then, history has leaders like Adolf Hitler who could impose his preconceived notion on others.

Thus, every leader differs from the other, but all of them carry the unique potential to influence others towards a specific goal. Leaders are mainly visionaries. They set the mission for an organization and, in turn, leads the whole of human resource towards attaining the goal.

Let me summarize a few chosen characteristics of good leadership:
- Leadership is an interpersonal process that revolves around the competency of influencing others.
- Intelligence, maturity, and personality are some of the essential ingredients of good leadership.
- It is a group process. No man is an island. Leadership happens within a group of people.
- Leadership is situation-bound. There is no best type of leadership that fits all. A leader's true potential is observed during duress.
- The role of a leader cannot be restricted to inspiration alone. They are indeed equipped with the task of deciding the destiny of high-performing teams.

The significance of leadership is justified by the following actions:

1. **Initiates Action:** Leaders start the work by communicating the organizational plan and policies.
2. **Motivation:** A leader's job is to motivate the team by not only showcasing the benefits of achieving the goal but also by playing an incentive role.
3. **Giving Guidance and Building Confidence:** A leader doesn't delegate the work and sits in his AC cabin.

A good leader guides the workforce, builds the confidence level of the team. His main role is to guide the team towards effective as well as efficient performance.

4. **Build Conducive Work Environment:** An employee's performance improves in a positive working ambiance. A leader's job is to ensure the presence of a conducive working environment.
5. **Coordination:** It is imperative for a leader to ensure that an employee's personal goal is met along with the organizational goal.
6. **Required at all Levels:** Leadership is a quality that should be implemented at all levels of management. At the top level, leaders decide on the policies, while at the middle management level, leaders supervise the execution of the set plans. Leadership works out at every level through appropriate guidance and counseling of the subordinates.

IS LEADERSHIP SAME AS MANAGERSHIP?

Difference between Managers and Leaders

Leaders	Managers
• ARTISTIC	• SCIENTIFIC SPECIFIC
• DREAMER	• SCEPTICAL
• OPTIMISTIC	• LOGICAL
• EMOTIONAL	• METHODICAL
• CHARISMATIC AND HOLISTIC	• FOCUS ON SYSTEMS AND PROCEDURES
• FOCUS ON PEOPLE	• USES AUTHORITY AND CONTROL
• USES INSPIRATION, INFLUENCE, AND EMPOWERMENT	• ADMINISTER
• PROACTIVE	• REACTICE
• ARE VISIONARIES	• SHORT TERM RESULTS
	• DELIVER
	• MISSIONARIES

The answer to the above question is an astounding NO. Leadership is NOT synonymous with Managership.

A leader doesn't require a managerial position to lead. However, a manager can be an effective one if he has the traits of a leader. I often encounter this question; what is the qualification or level expected from a leader? During one of my sessions with the administrative team of the company, an employee asked who could take up the role of a leader.

The question startled me at first, as leadership is a quality that is often associated with the top-level employees of any firm. However, the fact is hierarchy doesn't have a role in building leadership quality. One can be a first-time manager and still an excellent leader and can build a high-performing team. Leadership is a quality that anyone can adopt or develop. Whether one is a part of an SME or an MNC or a political organization, leadership is available for every seat. And this approach should be implemented in every kind of organization. Once each employee is allowed to own their job role, nurture the leadership quality, every team can transform into a high-performing team.

An organization's growth and destiny are assessed by five factors; Strategy, Organizational Structure, Operational Processes, Technological Products, and Finance. The leaders are entrusted with the duties of ensuring that these components are delivered to the right people at the right time. They play a crucial role in the overall development of the organization. I have seen many cases where brilliant strategies were developed for the products, but nothing bore the expected result.

In such cases, while introspecting this untoward depreciation, it was often found that the company either didn't have the right people for the right role, or the company had the right people, but they failed to act at the right time. In certain cases, leaders failed while implementing their personal agendas over the organization's goal, while in others, managers failed to garner the leadership skills to drive the team. A team or an organization can fail due to different reasons; nevertheless, a good leader can perform efficient conflict management at different stages to resurrect a high-performing team.

COMPETENCIES OF A LEADER

While deciphering the core competencies of a leader, one must ensure a balance of technical capabilities, functional capabilities, and soft skill capabilities.

Let's have a closer look at some of my experiences.

- **Knowing the Role:** This capability is especially required for first-time managers. However, no matter which tier one is serving, the role and responsibilities must be clear.

  Knowing the role and responsibilities ensures one analyzes how capable one is to lead the team. Many management gurus compare organizational teams with actors in a stage play. Each one is assigned a particular character to play. Similarly, knowing your role is the first step in the process of building leadership.

- **Having the Required Skill:** As revealed in the case study of the previous chapter, the leaders of the organization must possess the skills that the organization needs. There must be cohesion between the functional and technical skills of the leaders with that of the organization's operational process. A team of software engineers works more efficiently if the leader shares the same knowledge and skills. On the same note, one cannot expect a subject-matter expert. For example, to run a hotel industry, the head of finance needs not to know cooking. However, even if one is deprived of expertise in that particular field, one should have expertise in setting team goals, driving the team in achieving those goals, assessing the team's performance, and should remain aware of the SMART concept of goal management.

- **Provide Right Resources:** As stated earlier, leaders can never be self-oriented. They must guide and must come forward to help. Providing the right kind of resources is the first step to leading a team towards the set goal. You cannot set a software coding target without providing laptops, can you?

- **Authority:** Here, I shall give the example of M.K. Gandhi. He never held any political position; still, he remains one of the major leaders of India's freedom movement. When you hold a position of repute in an organization, you get a certain amount of authority to delegate the work. However, a leader can make a team high-performing by executing more of his informal authority. Delegate the work but do not control it. Add a human factor while exercising your leadership skills. Impart constructive criticism and show room for improvement.

- **Managerial Skill:** Here, I am not pointing at the kind of management degree one hold.

A team is an assortment of different age groups, people from different economic backgrounds. Managing different mindsets all at once is not everyone's cup of tea. It is indeed difficult.

Previous surveys have proved that first-time managers often have 60 to 70 percent technical skills and 30 to 40 percent soft skills. In contrast, the top management carries more soft skills. They are more equipped to handle a diversified team.

CONFLICT MANAGEMENT

"Conflict is good in a negotiation process. It is the clash of two ideas, which then, all being well, produces a third idea."- **Luke Roberts**.

Conflict is ubiquitous. Two brains never think alike, creating a conflict of ideas and even ideologies. Disagreeing is inherent to humans; nevertheless, disagreements are beneficial from an organizational point of view if handled correctly. Managing conflict is an essential trait of a good leader. A first-time manager is often adversely affected once exposed to conflicts. However, the capability of managing conflicts amongst the senior leaders is worth imitating. There are three main aspects of conflict management.

- Resolving conflicts amicably to promote a healthy working environment.
- Developing and inspiring others to follow a particular style that can reduce the chances of a conflict.
- Nurture the ability to manage teams having different levels of capabilities and willingness.
- Every conflict comes with its own terms and conditions. No one size fits all. Conflicts can be managed in different ways, either emulating a repressive condition or a compromising condition. Amicably addressing a conflict enhances a healthy working culture, whereas repressive management often triggers the problem to recur. Most leaders often tend to proclaim the style that they use for managing conflicts. In fact, they often forget that learning by seeing or imitating has more effect than learning by listening to continuous lectures. Hence, leaders should make a point to show their style and be a model for the employees, rather than just being verbose. Conflicts can metamorphose into any shapes and forms.

- A good leader must fathom the situational demands and then chalk out an appropriate plan of conflict management.

STYLES OF CONFLICT MANAGEMENT

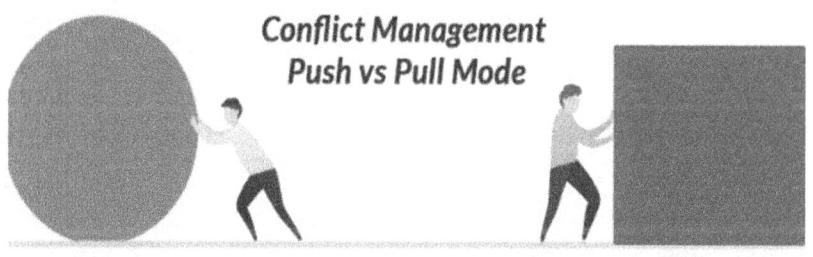

Persuasive Style

Values: Logic, rationale, data, numbers, information

Proposing
Suggesting, putting forward, advising, offering, recommending

Reasoning
Proving, explaining, showing, indicating, arguing, discussing, debating (facts)

Visionary Style

Values: Logic, rationale, data, numbers, information

Articulating
Describing, creating, painting, appealing, portraying, recounting, depicting, relating, representing

Inspiring
Exciting, arousing, stimulating, activating, urging, invigorating, provoking, animating

Assertive Style

Values: Personal rights and others rights

Demanding
Needing, wanting, requiring, claiming, desiring, craving, stating, expressing, exerting

Providing Incentives and pressures
Bargaining, negotiating, exchanging, trading, settling, dealing

Participative Style

Values: Sharing feelings, emotions, personal issues

Disclosing
Sharing, admitting, divulging, revealing, uncovering, exposing exerting

Listening
Empathizing, paraphrasing, reflecting, summarizing, clarifying, attending, questioning

1. **Persuasive Style**: Here, the leader tries to tone down the situation by persuading them with logical facts, quantitative data, and other valid information.

Open discussions or debates are entertained in such a style where the following points are taken care of.

Through organized data and valid information, suggestions are proposed while having a healthy argument.

2. **Assertive Style**: As the name implies, it indicates stating your views and standing your ground without compromising your perspective or value system. It is not about being inflexible but demonstrating a clear thought perspective expressed in a polite but firm manner.
3. **Visionary Style**: It is one of the best styles of conflict management. The goal here is to focus on one's own identity and make it inspiring for others. The individual here is capable of seeing and showing others the bigger picture. The leader carries an immense power of articulating the organizational purpose in a more appealing way.

   The leader induces a slice of excitement, motivation, and desire to perform towards the bigger goal.
4. **Participative Style**: In such a mode, the leader is inclusive of his people and enables them to share or voice out their opinion and participate actively. This is a sort of democratic way of leading and can be a highly effective way to manage conflict.

   Empathizing, paraphrasing, reflecting, listening, and clarifying are some of the core values of the participative style of conflict management.

SITUATIONAL LEADERSHIP

With human and industrial evolution, the perception of leadership has evolved too. Still, leadership qualities remain an integral part of the organizational fabric.

A leader is not elected to avoid any impending harm. However, a leader is chosen to lead the team to walk through adverse situations. We entrust our leaders with ourselves. We believe they can stand still and lead us through, *no matter what.*

The most significant quality of a leader is to adapt to situational demands. A leader is the one holding the torch in the dark tunnel of obstacles. As John Maxwell quoted,

> *"Leaders must be close enough to relate to others, but far enough ahead to motivate them."*

The term *Leader* is about leading, not just dictating what to do. Considering the tasks, the way in which the tasks are delegated, the organizational relationship, the desire to perform, **let's explore situational leadership in detail.**

Task: The extent to which a leader engages in one-way communication by telling each follower what to do, when to do it, where, and how the tasks are to be accomplished.

Activities indicating task behavior are:
- Initiate structure by setting the rules and regulations.
- Define the targets clearly.
- Define direction.
- Set priorities

Relationship: The extent to which a leader engages in two-way communication, listening, providing socio-economic support, and facilitating. Activities indicating relationship behavior are:
- Consideration.
- Sharing Ideas/Seeking Suggestions.
- Counseling to motivate and develop subordination.
- Allowing certain freedom while deciding the modus-operandi for task completion.
- Concern for the well-being of the team.

Maturity: Refers to the level of maturity exhibited by a subordinate to execute a particular task.

This is measured on the basis of:
- The ability (A) to carry out the task
- Willingness (W) to handle the task

The various maturity levels are:
- M1 - Low A/ Low W
- M2 - Low A/ High W
- M3 - High A/ Low W
- M4 - High A/ High W

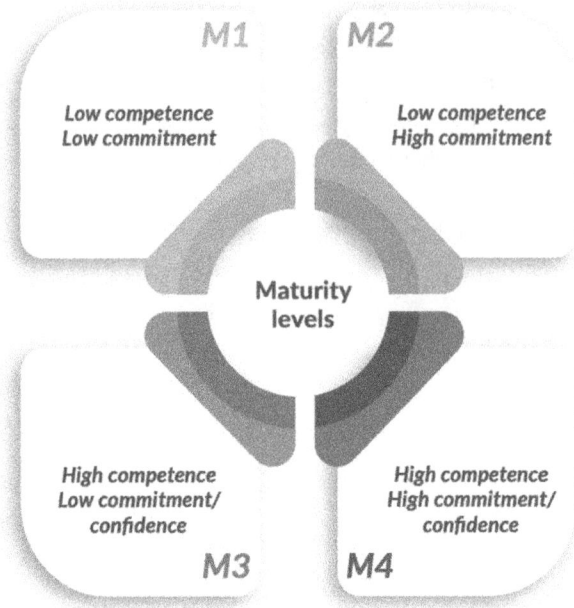

There are four different styles of Situational Leadership.
1. **Telling style**: The flow here is from the leader to the teams. Most decisions are made based on the timely and effective completion of projects.
   They have moderate to high amounts of Task Behavior and moderate to low amounts of Relationship Behavior.
2. **Selling style**: This style is high both in terms of task and behavior. While the leader is still in control of the tasks, there is still a chance to discuss and communicate the flexibility and flow of it with the employees.
3. **Participating style**: This style is high in terms of relationship but low in terms of the task. We can consider this style to be the contrast and opposite of the telling style. It is driven entirely by the team rather than by the leader. There is a chance for them to interact, discuss and decide the flow and completion of a task.
4. **Delegating task style**: It is low in terms of both relationship and task. The flow here is from the team to the leader. The individual is considered capable enough to do the task without the involvement of the leader.

There are certain points to keep in mind. As the level of maturity of the follower increases, the leader's intrusion should reduce in the task behavior and increase in relationship behavior. For an average level of maturity, it is imperative for the leader to start reducing relationship behavior. At a high maturity level, there is minimal use of both tasks as well as relationship behavior.

CASE STUDY:

This is the happiest day of life for Abraham King, a Sales Manager with Excellent Life Insurance Company Ltd. He has just been chosen as The Sales Manager of the Year for the period of April 2001 to March 2002.

His success can be attributed to his excellent man-management skills.

Let's illustrate through four of his Life Advisors.

Mrs. June Ray:
- A housewife who has become a Life Advisor as her husband wanted her to do some constructive work instead of spending time at home.
- June does not have any previous work experience and does not seem to be too keen to learn the business of selling Life Insurance.

Mr. Rush Soon:
- Rush is a bright young MBA graduate with one year of sales experience in an FMCG organization.
- Rush is a very keen learner but has never sold Insurance earlier.
- After attending 100 hours of training, Rush has acquired product knowledge but is unable to sell effectively.

Ms. Easy Braganza:
- Easy has been a Life Advisor for the last year.
- Initially, Easy was performing well and was able to clock 20 policies in six months.
- Easy is knowledgeable about Excellent Life Insurance Company products and has fairly good communication and influencing skills.

- She has not sold any policies for the last six months and has started losing interest as she experiences delays in getting her proposal forms cleared from operations.

Mr. Tom Dependable:
- Tom has been one of the most successful Life Advisor in Abraham's Team.
- Tom has a sound knowledge of the product, effective communication skills, tremendous initiative, and drive.
- Tom is the best Life Advisor in Abraham's team and has been the most consistent performer.

To ensure the best results through the above-mentioned Life Advisors, Abraham adopted the following approach:

Mrs. June Ray:
Abraham had a personal discussion with June and mentioned that if she were unable to clock at least 5 policies in a month, it would be unviable for her to continue with the organization as a Life Advisor. However, considering June's inexperience in the field, Abraham spent time coaching June on areas pertaining to planning her day, making telephone calls, handling objections, and formalizing the number of appointments to be made per day. He also supervised her at periodic intervals.

With Abraham's effort, June started clocking in 6 policies a month.

Mr. Rush Soon
Abraham made joint calls with Rush. At the end of each call, they analyzed the cause of success and rejection while emphasizing Rush's strengths and areas of improvement. In addition, Abraham spent at least two hours a week with Rush to jointly review progress and get inputs on additional support areas as Rush needed. He encouraged Rush to express his concerns freely during these meetings. Abraham's input equipped Rush with the necessary skills to clock 8 policies per month.

Ms. Easy Braganza
Abraham spent time with Easy, trying to ascertain the reason for Easy's present level of performance.

Easy expressed her concerns over the procedural delays from the Operations, which were causing resentment to her clients. Abraham also assured Easy that he would personally follow up with the proposals that needed speedy clearances. With such reassurance, Easy got back to her usual performance level and clocked 25 policies in the next 6 months.

Mr. Tom Dependable

Abraham followed a hands-off approach with Tom and would only contact him occasionally to share information on products/competition and to enquire if Tom needed any support from him. Tom continued to perform well and clocked a policy of a well-known film star for Rs 5 crore sum assured.

So, what are the leadership approaches we spot in this case?

With Ms. June, Abraham used the telling style. He moved on to the selling style with Mr. Rush, participating style with Ms. Easy Braganza, and finally, the delegating style with Mr. Tom. As we see, Mr. Tom was the most successful of the four. The complete freedom and trust that Abraham had entrusted Tom with were worth it.

However, Tom's maturity level was kept in mind, and he was prompted every now and then to make sure he had everything he needed. A good leader is the heart and soul of a high-performing team. Without a leader, there is no hand to guide, motivate and inspire. And without these elements, there is no performance at all.

To conclude here, I'd like to leave you with two interviews with wonderful leaders who have been managing and leading high-performing teams for a while.

Let us understand different leadership perspectives and what leadership means to them.

EXCERPTS FROM INTERVIEWS OF CEO OF LEADING GLOBAL ORGANISATIONS:

Interview 1:

> **What would you define as a high-performing team?**

A high-performing team to me is the one that quantitatively achieves the given targets and qualitatively seeks to raise the bar in a consistent manner.

What are the key metrics to measure the team performance - how do you set the right performance standards?

Key Metrics to be measured are:
1) Target achievement – at an individual level as well as at the team level
2) Customer Focus
3) Practical Creativity/Innovation
4) Team Dynamics

What are the key criteria you leverage for?

- Hiring high performance
- A thorough and scientific recruitment process
- Developing high performance
- Consistent training and development programs
- Retention of high performers
- Exciting work challenges and charting out a mutually recognized career development plan.
- Motivating and engaging high performers
- Rewards and recognition

What are the key challenges faced by you while hiring, retaining, and developing high performers?

- Cost of hiring
- Keeping them challenged enough for a longer-term
- Organization's ability to keep pace with their ambition and growth path

How have you overcome challenges in Building high-performing teams?

Using a spirit of competition and celebrating achievements

What do you look for while identifying successors for your role?

Apart from the ability to perform tasks competently at my level, I look for an ability to challenge myself with a well-defined contrarian thought and a logical conviction to carry it through.

What strategies have you leveraged for building and sustaining virtual teams?

Regular and consistent communication to keep them connected and allay the fear of missing out.

What strategies do you leverage in building diversity and inclusion in your team?

We seek talent-based teams. Diversity and inclusion are derived as a by-product. Also, it's a bit function and task-specific. Some tasks demand homogeneity where diversity may not be leveraged, while in others, diversity may have leverage.

How do you create a high-performance culture in your team?

Recognizing and rewarding high performers and differentiating them from others is step one. Developing a 'critical next' layer consisting of high performers and investing in the development of their skills and competencies. Create a scope of work that challenges them and a clearly articulated career development plan which motivates them to look into the future.

Interview 2:

What would you define as a high-performing team?

A high-performing team is one that consistently achieves results and demonstrates consistency in performance. In my mind, a high-performing team needs to have people with complementary skills, where trust between the members is high.

They have an intuitive understanding of when to pitch in for each other. And all team members seamlessly move between leadership-followership roles based on their expertise.

What are the key metrics you use to measure team performance -how do you set the right performance standards?

The valence or reward has to be on the team performance rather than individual performance. Ultimately, teamwork can only happen when everyone feels an equal stake in the success of the team and is not individually led.

All parameters or metrics need to reward team performance and not individual performance.

Individual performance can be recognized or used to determine if someone should be on the team or not, but reward needs to be disproportionate, if not wholly linked, to team performance.

What are the key criteria you leverage for?

- *Hiring high performance – hire for attitude and intellect*
- *Developing high performance – High performers need to be challenged with stretch goals, so they need to be tested with challenging or complex assignments or job rotation. These are the best way to develop high performers on the job.*
- *Retention of high performers – Accelerated career progression*
- *Motivating and engaging high performers – career progression and recognition*

What are the key challenges faced by you while hiring, retaining, developing high performers?

- *High performers need challenging assignments and championing or mentoring support so they don't get derailed. It is important to keep high performers' feet firmly on the ground and not their heads in the air as it breeds arrogance and is self-destructive.*
- *Creating opportunities for growth and career progression ahead of time is linked to the growth of the business or vacancies.*
- *Encouraging risk-taking behavior and moving people away from their comfort zone.*

How have you overcome challenges in Building high-performing teams?

- *Policy of internal succession and growth from within*
- *Campus / cadre-based hiring program*
- *Differentiated career progression and reward based on merit*

What do you look for while identifying successors for your role?

There is no template model, but the 2 defining criteria for success are likeability and capability for the role.

What strategies have you leveraged for building and sustaining virtual teams?

> - *Regular interaction and engagement – higher intensity due to lack of physical proximity*
> - *One on one contact – check-in at regular intervals*
>
> **What strategies do you leverage in building diversity and inclusion in your team?**
>   a. *The first principle is a meritocracy and equal opportunity and a non-discriminatory policy framework.*
>   b. *Genuine intent to support inclusivity*
>   c. *Micro Targets*
>
> **How do you create a high-performance culture in your team?**
> - *Making everyone have a voice – stake in the success of the team*
> - *Discourage or draw a red line on any behavior that compromises the team performance*
> - *Give equal access to everyone- no one should feel too special or isolated.*

TAKEAWAYS:

- A leader's role includes directing, training, motivating, inspiring, and enhancing the team spirit.
- The Theory of Situational Leadership is based upon the task, relationship, and maturity.
- Maturity is a function of an individual's ability and willingness to carry out a specific task.
- Effective Leaders are with a large amount of style flexibility/style range and style adaptability.

11

COACHING

The interesting thing about coaching is that you have to trouble the comfortable and comfort the troubled.
— *Ric Charlesworth.*

Broken is beautiful. That phrase has so much meaning in it. None of us like anything that is broken, but the truth is we all have insecurities; we all have faults. But just stop for a second and think, do the broken pieces of a mirror not form the most beautiful pattern of light? All it takes for us is to look beyond the imperfections and embrace our flaws because we are nothing if not human at the end of the day.

All of us know the art of pottery; it is about unmolded mud that needs to be given shape. The fact that a shapeless blob of clay turns into a stunning shape under pressure, patience, and consistent effort is truly a miracle. There is another art form that I am reminded of here.

Kintsugi is the Japanese art of putting broken pottery pieces back together with gold. It is built on the idea that you can create an even stronger, more beautiful piece of art by embracing flaws and imperfections. Sometimes, a "perfect" piece of pottery is also cracked open and pieced back together with gold.

Every break is unique, and instead of repairing an item to make it look like it is new, the 400-year-old technique actually highlights the "scars" as a part of the design.

Using this as a metaphor for healing ourselves, we learn an important lesson: Sometimes, with the right amount of help, we can be made into something more unique and beautiful. Sometimes, being cracked open for improvement results in unleashing one's true potential. Often, the power of authority can blind us in ways where we are not even aware of being blinded, and many a time, this costs us dearly. There comes a time in life when we all have to self-inspect or self-reflect because self-doubt does more harm than good. And at these times, we might need a helping hand; this helping hand can be in the form of your coach or a mentor. When we look at coaching, we often tend to relate coaching more to global sports, and of late, this is also gaining momentum. In the business world, there are many business leaders who have appointed coaches. But what really is coaching?

Coaching is all about bringing about a positive change in people—helping you to uncover your latent potential, bringing it to the forefront, creating a path to identify your goals and look at various options to reach them, enabling you to understand your current reality, helping you achieve your goals and reach your potential, and creating a way forward. It is different from other helping or enabling methodologies, like counseling and therapy. Coaching believes in the principle that you have the answers within you. It is about the coach facilitating in uncovering a person's potential by playing the role of a catalyst.

A coach will ask you several questions, which will help you get the right answer and sustain those answers as principles. A coach will help you evaluate those answers and see what works best for you. A coach will help you create a way forward with a SMART (specific, measurable, attainable, results-oriented, and time-bound) approach. I previously stated that there are helping or enabling methodologies, like counseling and therapy. However, they are prescriptive methodologies that tell you what needs to be done. They are helpful in a different context. But coaching is a little different. A coach helps a client identify the current reality and look at it in a very neutral and unbiased manner. Coaching helps clients establish their strategy using various tools and options. These tools help identify the pros and cons or the merits and demerits of each option. They also aid the coach in guiding the client to choose the best option. How does coaching help you?

What kind of benefits can you expect out of coaching? You can not only expect benefits since it is highly customized to your environment, but you can also at once see changes in your thought process. This, in turn, helps you create the right strategy for success. Very often, when we put in a lot of effort, we end up doing so in the wrong direction because of a lack of guidance.

On the other hand, effective coaching helps you manage the changes and transition, initially within yourself, as it helps you lead and guide change in others. It creates a roadmap with which you can measure and see success for yourself. It helps you define your own measures of success.

All of this results not only in behavioral changes but also in very visible changes in performance for both the individual and the organization. We must have all heard the famous quote by John Wooden, "A good coach can change a game, a great coach can change a life." In our personal lives, we get coached on different things. Starting from our birth, we are taught to walk, we are taught to eat, and we are taught many skills that we need to survive. Once we have those skills, we are coached about things that are not essential for survival but necessary to excel in life. Sometimes due to our own mistakes or due to mediocre or shabby coaching, we find ourselves facing failures. But the level a good coach will help one reach is absolutely unmatched.

The role of a leader is to enhance the performance of the team by identifying their performance gaps, nurturing them, giving them timely feedback, and helping them acquire the right kind of skills and knowledge to perform roles effectively.

A leader acts as an unofficial coach. A big part of leading a team includes coaching as well as keeping the team motivated and encouraging and inspiring them to perform to the best of their ability. Instructor style is a method where a coach tells the 'coachee' what needs to be done; this typically works well where the coach provides very clear instructions and the person being coached or the client one is dealing with does not know what to do or how to do it. Leadership style is the mark of confident leaders who map the way and set expectations while engaging and energizing followers along the way.

In a climate of uncertainty, these leaders lift the fog for people. They help them see where the company is going and what is going to happen when they get there. Unlike instructors, coaches take the time to explain their thinking: They do not just issue orders. Most of all, they allow people the choice and latitude on how to achieve common goals.

So how do you coach as a leader? It starts with identifying the knowledge gap. When we talk about the knowledge gap, it means does the person know what needs to be done? Is the individual aligned with the tasks technically, functionally, or behaviorally? Measuring this will relate to job success. In other words, it is linked to an individual's technical, functional, and behavioral competencies.

So, identifying whether the individual has the right knowledge is crucial. Suppose the individual does not have the right knowledge. In that case, it is about imparting the right kind of knowledge to them from books: you can either refer to the right books and convey the information to the individual or directly recommend the book to them. One can also take advice from managers or participants who have attended training sessions and received certifications. The role of a manager is to help them translate the conceptual knowledge they have learned on the job to the team.

The next step is to ensure that individuals are self-motivated and inspired to achieve their goals. This is where a manager plays a role in contributing to the performance of the individual. Without motivation, individuals will not open their minds to learning. It is up to the leader to motivate them and prep them for all the learning that is coming their way. Be ready to go anywhere as long as it is in the forward direction. Let us explore the many benefits of coaching. Mainly, it provides a customized approach.

It helps create specific action plans which are customized to individual needs. Customization has its own benefits; it helps one align with the company's goals better. It minimizes the time period that is required to meet a goal. It defines clear measures and metrics of success. It also helps provide the right solution for the right issue, and it can and will give the maximum returns on investment to individuals. There are different ways of coaching that have developed over time.

Virtual coaching is now the most popular method of coaching in the workplace, given the Covid situation. Even before the recent spike in working virtually, organizations were becoming more global, virtual meetings were becoming more prevalent, and virtual coaching was in demand. This type of coaching has become totally commonplace, and all of the previously mentioned types of coaching in the workplace—executive, instructive, and team coaching—can be done virtually. Virtual coaching is an ideal option for teams from different countries and time zones, as well as for those interested in a coaching arrangement they can easily integrate into their hectic schedules.

Through videography, a virtual coach can engage with his audience and facilitate learning in the same manner that they would in a face-to-face setting. Additionally, the coach matching process is not limited to geographic and travel constraints, which often increases compatibility and flexibility. Now, there are four different methods of coaching, which filter the process even more. Every method comes with its own advantages. What matters here is what fits best to the sort of training you are hoping for.
Let us explore each method in detail.

Executive coaching: Executive coaching is where a coach works with an individual or a small group to help solve a business problem or align the individual's or the group's goals and creates action plans to solve a business problem. Top employees can also benefit from executive coaching.

Career transition coaching: This method of coaching helps where individuals are going through career transitions either as a student, where they are unclear about the career opportunities they should pursue, or as career professionals who want to make a career shift: working professionals may want to become entrepreneurs or entrepreneurs may be looking at diversification.

In addition, individuals who are transitioning to bigger and broader roles, such as an individual contributor becoming a first-time manager, a mid-level executive taking on a strategic role, or CEX or CXO moving into a CEO's role, could also benefit from career transition coaching.

Life coaching: Here, you work with individuals to solve their problems with life issues, where life issues could involve personal life goals, financial goals, or relationship goals. It could also be wellness goals. A life coach also takes note of the obstructions and limitations of a person's personal life and works on helping them overcome them. Life coaching is a form of talking therapy. It has proven to be highly influential in changing the lives of millions of people. Often, we do not know what we need until we start taking these sessions.

To lead a life just as we are, without our insecurities, fear, and anything holding us back is a beautiful concept and a dream to many. Life coaching can play a vital role in not just transforming your personal life but also your professional life.

Organization development coaching: Here, a coach works with individuals to solve a business problem. This can be either individuals or groups of teams that work toward solving a business issue.

The emphasis is on the business issue, but it may help in individual development as a byproduct. However, it definitely gives measurable results in organizational development. This sort of coaching usually focuses more on the people and change in terms of culture change and leadership abilities and usually helps in forming business strategies.

This coaching includes various methodologies and formats that aim to foster healthy interactions and achieve high performance. These may be fairly structured and prescriptive, such as during a retreat where a coach has worked with the team's leadership to create the agenda and then facilitates the meeting, possibly even teaching content sometimes.

There are so many roads with various destinations in life: how do you find your destination, and how do you choose your path? The road not taken is usually the one with the most beautiful destination. Same with coaches as well. To summarize,

- You first need to identify the need for coaching.
- Next, set the expectations from the coaching clearly and see that it aligns with the organizational requirements as well.
- Define beforehand how you are going to measure success as a result of the coaching. How often are you going to be engaging, and what is the level of commitment to be expected? That is, how frequently are you going to meet or talk or discuss? What are you going to discuss during those meetings? And how would you add the role of the coach as well as the coaching?
- Ensure that the sessions do not turn out to be mere brainstorming sessions due to a lack of familiarity with the concept of coaching.
- Make sure that all discussions lead to a commitment for action. The coach can leverage his position as a sounding board, a guide, or a mentor.

But at the end of the day, we have to agree that there has to be some action as a result of the coaching. And in subsequent sessions, we need to review whether those actions have been implemented by the 'coachee.' What was their experience in implementing them?

If the actions have not been implemented, what has stopped people from doing so? And what have been some of the challenges that they faced, and how can we navigate or overcome those challenges?

This accountability holds true whether a person is into executive coaching, life coaching, wellness coaching, or organization development. These guiding principles or steps are helpful in all types of coaching.

CASE STUDY:

I have been coaching the CEO of a $1 billion enterprise. The background of this person is that he has worked with the organization for close to two decades and has very strong academic credentials. He had built the organization from close to a $1 million enterprise to a 1-billion-dollar enterprise that came from organic and inorganic growth. It is a profitable organization, and the CEO is a person with a very strong operational and tactical background and orientation. I would say he had the ability to think strategically but could not communicate strategic thinking to the team and was not able to build the right kind of inclusive culture in the organization. This created a gap between him and his team members. The CEO's leadership style came in from a view of organizing and the view of actually driving the growth of the business.

At that point in time, the CEO was having a lot of self-doubts, which all of us experience at one time or another, although most of us are not very vocal about it. The CEO continued to be passionate about the business and continued to believe in the future of his business because, of course, hope is really the last thread we cling to in life. He was truly committed to delivering what needed to be delivered, and there was also a sense of engagement in driving the business forward.

So, at this juncture, this was the situation. The CEO was beginning to be a little uncomfortable. He was experiencing self-doubt about whether his leadership style was the right one to lead the organization forward. As a coach, I had to help him reflect: to help him work on specific gaps, for, after all, we are all humans, are we not? The necessary had to be done, but how? I started with RTT (real-time text) conversations with the CEO, including having breakfast, snack, lunch, and dinner meetings. I had to look at the CEO's reports for psychometric reports. I also took the CEO through a lifeline exercise where the person plotted the highs and lows of their personal and professional careers, which helped me understand the CEO.

I looked at the situations the CEO had been through in his life professionally and personally. And from the data of psychometric reports, the life journey exercise, which I was talking with him, and also sharing information on the challenges and the strategic vision of his business, I was able to identify the goals that the CEO wanted to accomplish both from an organizational perspective and a personal perspective.

I also identified the motivators that drove the individual and the factors that called him. I was able to assess the purpose of doing what he was called to do. I was able to identify the specific gaps that required to be scrutinized. I also looked at 360-degree reports. And I also studied the composition of his direct reports, as well as that of some other members of the board. So, this helped me arrive at a comprehensive view of what needed to be done and how it needed to be done.

Finally, I had a discussion with the CEO, and we identified three potential barriers. And we started working to abolish them. The first step was ensuring that the CEO is able to look at strategy beyond only numbers and is able to create a compelling vision for the future.

Second, he is able to build an inclusive leadership style where he can engage different members of the leadership team and facilitate the executive team to drive business decisions and own them. And the third, that he is able to build a sense of purpose and eventually look at hiring a successor or getting a strong second line. We were able to cover a very specific plan, which was a two-year engagement. One person worked with the CEO on a monthly basis. He had to connect with the CEO throughout.

We also reviewed action plans. I also sat through some of the key business meetings and again offered feedback to the CEO about his performance and how well he was doing. This is what he was probably not doing before. So, when I had put in a period of about six months of coaching, the CEO's style became more inclusive.

The CEO was able to draw on ideas from the team, leverage his own ideas and insights, advance consultant standard ideas, leverage the board insights, and consolidate all of these toward a meaningful purpose. That meaningful purpose was effectively communicated to all the team members through the leadership team; it was communicated even to the grassroots level, right up to the individual contributors. So, everyone was aligned to a common set of objectives and a common sense of purpose. This helped to clear a lot of self-doubts experienced by the CEO.

He was able to align his heart, mind, and purpose together, and that helped him immensely in driving the business forward. AWS (Amazon Web Services) helped him to now measure success by measuring changes in leadership style, which came through strategic influence.

Second, he has now adopted a more inclusive style of engaging his leadership team. And the way he did this was through one-on-one discussions, group discussions, and empowering the leadership team to make certain decisions.

Last but not least, it is really effective to have open and authentic communication with your team members, and at times even let them see your vulnerable side. It is important to recognize that all humans have shortcomings, and one should be able to open up and say, "This is what the situation actually is, and this is where I need help."

These things helped the CEO tremendously; however, one cannot forget that the CEO was highly committed as well. He was ready to do anything it took. He paid serious attention to all the coaching input I provided as a part of the exercise for 24 months. He was not only able to show a top-line 80% CAGR (compounded annual growth rate) growth in the business, which is more than the industry rate of growth but was also able to increase the EBITDA (earnings before interest, taxation, depreciation, and amortization). We were able to identify a successor internally and groom the successor to take over his role.

This led to a strong sense of purpose and satisfaction to the CEO that not only had he contributed to driving top-line growth as the CEO, but he was also leaving a sustainable organization behind him. He has the right successor who will take the organization to the next level. The good part is, he did not have to look for a successor from outside the organization.

All of us have flaws and imperfections; that is what makes us human. Embracing it is one thing but working on it is another. Often, we do not realize that we need coaching or that there is some shortcoming in us.

We do not need coaching just because we lack something; sometimes, coaching helps us become better versions of ourselves. Coaches do play a major role in this journey.

Coaches help us think critically and creatively. When we have been at our jobs for a while, it is all too easy to adopt a stagnant mindset. We are comfortable doing business the way we always have. Confident leaders hire people better than themselves.

Employees who feel challenged and rewarded are less likely to leave and are more productive. Employee retention and productivity are key factors to business success—companies spend millions every year devising schemes to keep employees on the side. Frequently we hear that opportunity for growth and personal development are two of the biggest reasons high performers stay where they are. Offering business coaching to high-performing employees could be a huge incentive.

When you have an expert coach who will challenge your business acumen, you will learn which decisions might be reckless and which are founded on evidence-based decision-making. This is not to suggest that coaches can see into the future, but they will be able to identify whether you have assessed a potentially risky move from all angles and help you make a timely decision.

A stone that a sculptor sculpts can either remain as a stone or turn into a beautiful statue. That is all coaching is about, for one to be better and do better.

TAKEAWAYS:

- Set clear goals.
- Identify the root cause of the issue very clearly.
- Get the engagement and alignment of the CEO of the coaching with the 'coachees.' Define clearly, what are the expectations? What is it that the coaches would do and work with the coach? Review periodically and give honest, open, and authentic feedback. This will help drive transformational results in individuals. And when the 'coachees' experience success as a result of the coaching, you would have helped them achieve their business goals.
- There are various coaching styles and methods that can be customized according to the needs of the organization or individual.
- Executive coaching helps an individual look inwards by asking the right questions. A coach works with an individual or a small group to help solve a business problem and align the individuals' goals and create action plans to solve a business problem.
- Career transition coaching is a guiding hand that helps you to understand what roles suit your key strengths and abilities.

- Life coaching helps one's life, relationship, and financial goals. Transforming your personal life is essentially the first step in transforming your professional life.
- Organizational development coaching trains a set of individuals to leverage leadership abilities, culture, and strategies of the organization. This does not necessarily benefit individual growth but definitely benefits the organization.

12

BUILDING A LEADERSHIP PIPELINE AND SUCCESSORS

The challenge of leadership is to be strong but not rude; be kind, but not weak; be bold, but not bully; be thoughtful, but not lazy; be humble, but not timid; be proud, but not arrogant; have humor but without folly.
—Jim Rohn

History is not what it was, but what it is. So said William Faulkner, the American writer. We all love a good story; in fact, a lot of us have a favorite dynasty and favorite king and queen as well. The story I remember here is of the King shivaji. While **Chhatrapati Shivaji** is the founder of the Maratha Empire, it was under Peshwa that it expanded greatly. The empire ruled greatly from 1674-1818. Shivaji is known to be one of the greatest leaders in history.

We have to remember his administrator Dadoji Konddeo who played a huge role in his journey as a leader, to make up for the absence of Shivaji's father.

This could easily have been the inspiration behind Shivaji's motive to introduce peshwas, who could further expand the kingdom. Shivaji was an ideal leader who was prepared for any situation.

At the age of 16, he had his first victory when he captured Torna fort.

From there on, he has successful attempts at capturing many other forts and kingdoms. He didn't intend to overthrow a king or war against a kingdom and win power, but to bring a significant change in society. He wanted the better for his people.

From the very beginning of the age, his mother brought him up as someone who wouldn't differentiate between castes or religions, so it was understood that he wanted to leave the place better than it was when he found it. That is the intention that made him an inspiring leader who drove purpose.

Under his reign, well trained, strong set of army flourished. He even commanded and disciplined over 200 warships. The Maratha navy is known to have influenced the expansion of the Maratha empire. Shivaji not only founded an empire but also trained the men enough to expand it, gathered enough resources, built forts, captured forts, and finally established all the measures to ensure that the show goes on even after he steps down.

The importance of building a leadership pipeline and successors is often spoken about, and while the need is appreciated, not too many organizations do enough about it. The risks of not building a leadership pipeline are high and could effectively collapse any given organization in seconds. There are three types of risks involved here:

1. Strategic risks: These include not having the right people in the right roles at the right time to run your business. A vacuum at the head of the organization can be disastrous.

However much we talk about technology and however much we talk about products, essentially it is people who drive businesses. Therefore, not having the right people with the right skills at the right time has a direct impact on the top line and bottom line, not only for the current but also for the future. It also comes in the way of implementation of strategic planning.

2. Tactical risks: So, when we talk about some of the tactical risks, it is again about not having the right skills at the right time. We saw that strategic risks involve not having the right kind of leaders or having an inconsistent strategy. Tactical risks involve not having highly engaged teams to drive the organization into the future. Very often, I have noticed that a change in leadership in large global corporates means a change in virtually the entire leadership team. This creates an undue disruption of the business, elite stability, and unnecessary or undue anxiety in taking tactical risks.

This, in turn, impacts tactical decision-making in the corporate, which could involve commercial decisions, people decisions, production decisions, or customer decisions. This disruption in decision-making in the organization can backdate the business.

3. Operational risks: These are in terms of not having or building a leadership pipeline.

The key question is while these risks are here, there are businesses that have lost a lot of money. They have lost their market share and their reputation, largely because they did not have the right kind of succession plan or talent or leadership. The other issue is there is excessive reliance on one leadership style. We all are aware of situations, be it in political leadership or in business leadership, where there is a very high dependence on one individual. Everything revolves around this individual. And after the individual either retires or moves on, there is no one to continue the legacy. This is very often the scenario.

We have heard of empires disintegrating largely because of inadequate or incorrect succession planning, and history has been a witness to this. We have seen businesses disintegrate for the same reason. We have also witnessed political leadership and political parties fall apart because of a lack of leadership and not having a strong leadership pipeline. What are some of the key benefits of building a leadership pipeline, and what are the constraints? One, it builds sustainability. It ensures the continuity of strategy to execution and sustained development of the organization, whether it is a political, business, or social organization. Also, it does ensure seamless execution. It builds credibility with clients and successes when they know that the business is not person-dependent. These are some of the key benefits of succession planning.

So, now let us explore why organizations are lacking in putting leadership pipelines in place despite knowing all the benefits of doing so. The first reason I would like to highlight is the lack of serious focus. People like to make businesses and political parties person dependent; this could be on account of the company's own insecurity, personal insecurity, or having an attitude that the world revolves around me; thinking beyond these ideas is very critical to developing a strong talent pipeline.

Let us see the example of a very large global corporate that was into infrastructure.

The company had a leader who had been the chairman of the company for more than 30 odd years and helped in the growth of the business, but he had not done enough to build a strong second line.

The leader wanted to be in the chair for a very long time, and although well past the age of retirement, the person was not willing to let go of the reins. Even the assurance of adequate remuneration did not move him to relinquish the leadership position. Naturally, that eventually came in the way of developing a business for the future. This leader encouraged us in a very subservient style of leadership. Although the organization was doing well, it was not able to retain its market share position. It was a large global organization, but unfortunately, the individual leading the company was focused more on generating wealth for himself rather than on building an organization that would survive beyond him.

The second reason is about hiring for current skills and not potential. Here, I can talk about another large technology or business process management company, which had a very strong family legacy backup. However, they clearly did not do well because they had major issues in terms of increasing the company's market share as well as increasing its size, scale, and scope of business. Meanwhile, their competitors were growing at two to three times their current growth rate. This organization did not keep pace.

One of the key challenges, in this case, was a very tenured CEO, who was operationally relevant, and who had a leadership style that worked well in an operation environment but was not strategically oriented. And the second impediment was the CHRO, who hired people according to his personal preference. Again, a technology-experienced CHRO and a CEO end up hiring mediocre people, particularly to suit their pockets.

They hired people who are nice and polite but not necessarily the most capable. As a result, attrition at leadership levels was very high, which caused not only a loss of market share but also a major loss in terms of credibility with clients because clients kept asking, "why do you have a frequent change in leadership?". It is natural to be curious, even suspicious. It also caused a lot of ripples in the minds of employees. Especially when they had a new boss every two years to report to, it meant a sudden change in strategy.

This resulted in the new strategy becoming the focus of the company, and something that was initiated by the predecessor was all of a sudden stopped.

This frequent change in leadership also meant that the new people brought their own new teams to work under them. So, there was no continuity of leadership. In turn, this resulted in the business not growing and a loss of credibility in the market. And when they started acquiring, when there was a new CHRO after the previous CHRO retired, they found it very difficult to hire the right people in the organization.

So, this is an example of how individual styles, preferences, and biases come in the way of building succession. As for hiring for current skills, I have very often noticed that organizations do not have a process for assessing leadership potential, or even if they do have a process, they do not perform it thoroughly enough. They usually end up hiring for experience and only for current status, but not for potential leadership roles in the future. Therefore, when there is a gap at the level above, it invariably means that these organizations do not have anyone to take over these positions, and they have to get in the market to hire senior leaders, which is not the best strategy.

A lot of organizations like Unilever and ICICI in India hire leaders at the entry-level and then groom them using a combination of job rotations, coaching, mentoring, and giving challenging assignments and stretched responsibilities, which eventually makes them succession ready. In fact, the track records of these organizations, whether it is Unilever, India, or ICICI Bank, India, both large global corporates, show that they have leaders who are homegrown.

So, these CEOs who are typically starting their careers with these new organizations have already been through various job locations and have successfully navigated them before they were considered for the leadership positions. The organizations did not have to hire anybody from the outside. This is why these organizations have a strong market positioning, strong client base, and their own credible brand presence. The other thing is a lack of a defined strategy for succession planning. When we talk about succession planning and developing an integration pipeline, it is looked upon as an initiative with a box to be ticked rather than as a clear strategic intervention. It is one of the most important pillars of HR strategy and business strategy.

Therefore, when ownership is not filled right at the very top, the CEO does not own the strategy and delegates it purely to the HR department.

In such a situation, there will be no succession planning based on building a strong talent pipeline, and neither will this be ingrained in the culture of the organization.

The strategy on developing a leadership pipeline will flow to interventions and then subsequently into process renewal culture.

It virtually translates into a hybrid, where organizations go wrong. This is taken as an intervention. And that intervention gets lost when there is a change in government, either in terms of an HR or the CEO. This succession planning works if only it becomes a part of the culture and the DNA of the organization.

The other important criteria are around effective promotions, that is, promoting the right people for the right reasons and the right goods. Promotion is based purely on performance in the current job and very rarely is potentially considered. Even for a potential to be considered, it is left to a lot of subjective inputs by a line manager or sometimes maybe a strict level manager. Often it is based on individual likes and dislikes and individual perceptions rather than capability. A number of public sector undertakings in India also have a formalized Assessment Centre for promoting people at various levels. Here, we are talking about building a succession pipeline both for managerial roles as well as technical expertise.

Hence, when it comes down to managerial bench strength, what you need is a competency framework. This competency framework should be relevant to your business. It should be progressive, and it should be relevant not only for today, but it should also have clear behavioral indicators which measure performance. Moving on, what are the body defining roles for succession and developing a leadership pipeline? There are three critical roles which one needs to factor. There could be technical roles, which are high-impact roles for the business. For example, the actuarial role in the insurance industry requires high technical competence, or the coloring workforce or the coloring worker in the paint industry or the textile industry is again a highly skilled person. The role of a tea taster in the tea industry is a highly technical role, which also has a high business impact. So, these are critical roles for which you need to look at succession secondaries who are highly skilled or competent. This is especially crucial for critical leadership roles, whether they are at a strategic level or at a tactical level, which ensures either creation of strategy or successful implementation of strategy and third change agents who will either be leading transformation in the business or will be leading, guiding, or influencing change.

So, these are three critical roles which one should look at in terms of building a strong succession instinct.

Let us now discuss competency. In terms of competencies, it is extensively talked about when one is looking at succession planning, especially for leadership roles and change agent roles. Here, leadership competencies remain the main focus. But for technical roles, I have rarely come across any organization which assesses technical capabilities. It is also worth defining technical competencies for every role. Those technical competencies should be graded into three levels: beginner, practitioner, and expert.

Beginner means having basic skills, practitioner means capable of performing to the current level, and expert means capable of being seen as a role model or a benchmark, not only internally but also in the industry. Certain skills may require to be operating at a minimum practitioner level, but certain skills will be required to the demonstrated at an expert level. Therefore, one needs to be grading competencies, whether they are technical competencies or they are leadership competencies. Hence, this is a key area on which one needs to be focusing.

Moving on to the crucial element here, how do you create competencies?

You create them by:
- Looking at the business strategy,
- Looking at the organizational structure.
- Looking at work levels and roles.
- Having focus group discussions with key members, key role holders, and their managers, as well as the chat function, to see what drives successful behaviors and what are the necessary knowledge levels, skill levels, and behaviors they need to exhibit not only for the current level but also for the next level.

A competency framework usually covers three levels of leadership:
- Leaders of an Enterprise (CEO minus one level, i.e., CXO and Board level)
- Leaders of a Function (CXO minus one)
- Manager of Managers (CXO minus two)

Under normal circumstances, this would be a two-day Development Center involving a succession plan based on the 9-Box Performance–

Potential Grid covering a group of 12 participants with 3–4 qualified and trained assessors.

The 9-box grid helps assess and analyze the performance of employees. It does so not only in terms of their current performance, but it also enables one to project their growth in the future. As we see in the illustration above, there are three categories: low, moderate, and high. Each employee can be scored based on their performance. Low-performance employees can be filtered out, moderate performance employees can use training and development, and high-performing individuals can receive sustaining programs that help them consistently perform in the same way.

9 BOX GRID

Potential	Low Performance	Moderate Performance	High Performance
High	"Potential Gem" High potential / Low performance	"High Potential" High potential / Moderate performance	"Star" High potential / High performance
Moderate	"Inconsistent Player" Moderate potential / High performance	"Core Player" Moderate potential / Moderate performance	"High Performer" Moderate potential / High performance
Low	"Potential Gem" High potential / High performance	"Potential Gem" Low potential / Moderate performance	"Potential Gem" Low potential / High performance

Performance

Similarly, they can also be categorized based on low, moderate, and high **potential.** When both categories are compared together, for example, if an individual has both low performance and low potential, the organization will most likely have to let them go. But an individual who has been graded as having low performance but high potential may deserve a chance in training and development. Next, we talk about some of the tools that are used to calibrate succession. The initial round of successors would be identified by the Management Council/and would need to be validated through a 2-day Development Centre, which would include the following:

Psychometrics Tools—Hogan Inventory to identify leadership strengths, derailers, and values.

- 360-degree feedback
- Lifeline exercise
- Business case simulations
- Competency-based interviews
- Roleplays
- Post Assessment Center, an Individual Development Plan which highlights Potential

Succession planning can be done by in-house talent reviews and talent boards. They identify potential internally. Secondly, you can also use an assessment center to look at succession planning where you use a combination of internal and external assessors or external assessors leveraging psychometrics.

There is psychometrics which talks about leadership strengths, leadership derailers, and the motives, values, and preferences. Then you can also leverage business simulations. They help you identify decision-making skills and cognitive skills like problem-solving and innovative thinking. Moreover, you can hold competency-based interviews, which will also help you assess your problem-solving and decision-making capabilities. The other factors that need to be looked at include innovation, lateral thinking, the ability to manage difficult situations, and the ability to manage people. Role-plays can give you a good orientation on the person's capability to negotiate client interactions and the ability to manage difficult people situations.

I remember during my time, we had created a career framework for a technology company, which showed two different paths. One was a technical career path, and the second was a leadership path. So, when a new entrant joined the organization, what did they have to do, from a knowledge perspective and a certification perspective? What kind of experiences did they need to have to get there? What kind of career moves and job rotations and assignments were required for them to get the job?

At every level, what were some of the key milestones which people needed to understand before they took on bigger and broader goals? These were important aspects. Let us explore another one of the tools which I have developed: the Potential–Aspiration grid. So, in addition to the nine-box grid, we can use this grid to focus on aspirations since the 9-box grid focuses mostly on performance and does not take account of the aspirations.

The Potential–Aspiration grid takes into account the potential and the aspirations of the individual and gives you various strategies to deal with people having varying levels of potential and aspiration.

People can possess different levels of aspirations and different levels of potential, as explained in the grid. Those with high potential and high aspirations will typically be your fast trackers. The others can be assets for the organization. It is important that they are provided with enough opportunities for accelerated growth and also impress upon them the need to invest in their own development. You will also have people who have high potential and medium aspirations.

It is worth investing in them. This involves not only providing opportunities for the right kind of accelerated growth and focusing on their development but also assigning the right roles to them, which are in alignment with their aspirations.

Often, high-potential people without aspirations may be asked to take on a particular role. It may even demotivate them in the long run. It is vital to not lose out on anyone with high potential, even if maybe they have lower aspirations. For this, they have to be given the right kind of roles. Therefore, for high potential low aspiration individuals, it is crucial to figure out what motivates them and ascertain that they are assigned to the right role to retain and engage them.

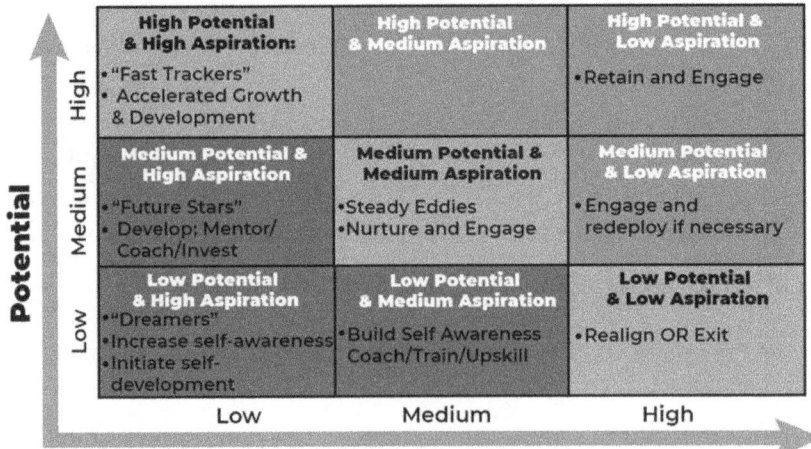

You should also focus on those with low potential and low aspirations. You either realign their roles or let them go. This is the right decision and can be helpful both for the individual as well as the business. How about persons with medium aspirations and low potential or high aspirations and low potential? The correct strategy for these employees would be to increase their awareness of themselves. Timely feedback and relevant coaching can bring them back to their element. Make them more self-aware and give them time to reflect on what they need to do.

Often lack of self-awareness is the main underlying issue in these individuals, and as soon as we are able to create self-awareness in them, we can focus on their development.

Many with low potential and high aspirations are recommended to attend coaching sessions. Let me cite the example of a candidate who felt they did not require coaching, although the organization was imposing very high aspirations on them. Clearly, there was no self-awareness in the candidate. The concerned candidate's argument was this: "Do I really need coaching? I bring so many years of experience to the table!"

Creating self-awareness in candidates involves the investment of sufficient time and effort on the part of the organization. This should continue until such time as when the candidates recognize their potential gaps and realize the steps they need to take for further development. The same principle holds true for creating self-awareness in candidates with low potential and medium aspirations as well.

Only when there is self-awareness can you focus on development. Development alone will not give you the right kind of results. Coming to people with high aspirations and medium potential, these candidates could be the future stars of the organization if you invest sufficient time in developing, mentoring, and coaching them. Those who have medium potential and medium aspirations are the 'Steady Eddies' of the organization. You need to look at the different ways in which you can keep them moving, motivated, and engaged and reward them based on their performance rate. It is important to adopt the appropriate strategy to engage them.

In succession planning, the right kind of development can be brought about on the job. This involves challenging people by giving them 'stretch assignments.' Stretch assignments are tasks that are beyond the person's current level of skills. They are usually focused on building a particular skill.

Often, I have seen individuals being given assignments that do not enable skill development but rather it is repetitive tasks, probably with some added-on complexity.

You need to focus on building skills by giving them opportunities to improve their current experience and state and acquire new skills.

Invest in mentoring and coaching these individuals. Whenever they are assigned additional responsibilities, they are bound to face some difficulties in completing them. In such situations, it is vital to have an internal mentor who can work with them or an external coach who can help with such critical tasks. I think, at present, we are neither investing enough time nor investing enough in resources like installing coaches. Having an external coach assigned when a person is transitioning either into a new role or a bigger role within the organization, or where a person from outside has been hired to succeed in your organization can bring about a tremendous gain in areas of skill development. There is an argument that, at senior levels, it is normally taken for granted that people will be successful in their new roles.

However, we have seen several instances of leadership failure at the C-suite levels (CEO, CFO, COO, and CIO) because of not integrating well culturally. Often, when leadership biases come into play in the hiring process, a few gaps in knowledge and skills in the candidate may be overlooked.

At times, the new individual coming from outside may need to have an external sounding board. This can aid them in bouncing their ideas and also help them come up with newer ways and different ways of integrating into the organization. A new person is usually hired to bring in change. An external coach brings in an element of neutrality, which can function as a different lens, rendering a different point of view. This is far better than being bogged down by an internal mentor. However, an ideal situation would be where the successor to the role has the help of the internal mentor as well as an external coach. This arrangement can go a long way in making the candidate successful. I would suggest a minimum duration of 6 to 12 months engagement for hiring an external coach. After a year, the transition becomes smooth, although, at times, it can happen earlier and faster. But organizations need to do enough to engage an external coach.

In addition, to make the endeavor successful, I think one needs to define the measures of success beforehand clearly. Define three or four critical areas you want to improvise. Or chalk out three or four goals you are looking to achieve for both the coach and the candidate.

And third, review the process periodically and do not postpone it. Periodic reviews help in highlighting any major or big-ticket concerns or issues early on and more easily so that you can take proactive steps to rectify the situation.

This helps to identify flaws in the candidate–role relationship early and prevents a situation where you realize that the relationship is not working months down the line.

To summarize, I would say the early investment will likely save the organization, probably millions of dollars at the C-suite level. And this is where I have seen organizations excel. There is no success without a successor. The above statement is self-defining on how important it is to have a successor, but is it an easy task to find one? Of course not, but neither is it impossible to find one. Here are some listed ways in which a successful successor can be chosen.

- Phase 1 of this mission includes the design of a leadership competency framework for CXO's and senior leadership.

  This phase would involve getting a holistic overview of the current business strategy, Target Operating Model of Hardware, the challenges, and the complexities of their respective domain through one-on-one discussions with the CEO, management council teams, and senior HR teams. This would be followed by a one-day group workshop where leadership competencies for succession planning and leadership development would be agreed on and behavioral indicators established to review performance. A one-day offsite workshop would be recommended.

- Phase 2 includes the succession planning and development center. Design of a competency framework covering three levels of leadership, that is, Leaders of an Enterprise (CEO minus one level—CXO and Board level), Leaders of a function (CXO minus one), and Manager of Managers (CXO minus two). This would be a two-day Development Center involving a succession plan based on the **9-Box Performance–Potential Grid covering a group of 12 participants with 3-4 qualified and trained assessors.**

- Now that the successor is chosen, the next ideal step has to be how to provide executive coaching for the successor?

Leverage executive coaching for the identified successors as per the Individual Development Plan customized to make their succession ready.

- There would be 12 sessions—one session per month for 3 hours each. Areas for coaching would include Strategic thinking, Innovation mindset, Building a high-performing team, Emotional Intelligence, Conflict handling, Leadership/Executive presence, Building an inspiration style, and Commercial and business orientation.

Finally, let us conclude this chapter like how we began; with the story of Shivaji Maharaj. The life story of Chhatrapati Shivaji Maharaj is the that never fails to inspire me. I'd like to remember not just his kingdom and the kingdoms he defeated, but his legendary leadership that is timeless and an inspiration for many like us. Shivaji Maharaj not only led and inspired noble causes, but he also understood the importance of leaving a line of successors behind him to rule and expand his kingdom.

He was a visionary, and more importantly, a revolutionary person who brought in the idea of ministerial government or 'Peshwai' who have continued to enable more leaders. The same can apply to leadership situations as well. Many people may come into power at some point in their lives, but if one does not know how to channelize the power and use it in the right direction, one cannot achieve a fruitful outcome or the desired outcome. Letting go of their reign and passing on the crown is an extremely difficult task for many leaders. Often, they get all embroiled in the trappings of wealth and position. But the fact to note here is leadership is not about position. Your success as a leader depends on how many more leaders you create and nurture. The success of your organization depends not on who leads it but where it is headed. History repeatedly teaches us where and why we go wrong, and we would do well to learn from it. We ought not to write the same chapter repeatedly but rather aim to write a new chapter that is entirely ours. Are you ready to write a new chapter?

TAKEAWAYS:

- The success of an organization depends not only on leaders but also on leadership pipelines.

- The risks of not building a leadership pipeline involve strategic, tactical, and operational risks, all of them being of equal importance.
- To develop a leadership pipeline and successors, one needs to assess their employees thoroughly.
  The 9-box grid and the potential–aspiration grid can be of great value here.
- Other than those with low potential, performance, and aspiration, employees should be invested in training and development.

PART C:
MAINTAINING HIGH PERFORMANCE TEAMS

13

CREATING HIGH PERFORMING VIRTUAL TEAMS

"You should never view your challenges as a disadvantage. Instead, it's important for you to understand that your experience facing and overcoming adversity is actually one of your biggest advantages." – Michelle Obama.

On January 27th, 2020, a 20-year-old woman presented to the Emergency Department in the General Hospital, Thrissur, Kerala, with a one-day history of dry cough and sore throat. There was no history of fever, rhinitis, or shortness of breath. She disclosed that she returned to Kerala from Wuhan city, China, on January 23rd, 2020, due to the Covid-19 outbreak there. She was asymptomatic between January 23rd and January 26th.

On the 27th morning, she felt a mild sore throat and dry cough. She did not give a history of contact with a person suspected or confirmed with Covid-19 infection. She had not visited the Huanan Seafood Wholesale Market; however, she gave a history of travel from Wuhan to Kunming by train. She had noticed people with respiratory symptoms in the railway station and on the train. The Kerala state government health authorities instructed her to visit a healthcare facility if she developed any symptoms because of the travel history to China and then and there *began a new era*.

Paradoxically, India conceives the first image of COVID-19 with migrant laborers lugging their belongings and walking miles and miles. India's labor market's fragility became open to the world with most of the economy shut down. Almost 10 million people returned to their villages, where half a million of them walked or cycled.

The people in the urban areas who had stayed back had a strong urge to connect, but the question was how. The initial few days of the imposed lockdown were tough, and people were scared for their lives. How was the gap to be bridged? Digitalization was our one and only option. We now live in the pandemic world, as well as a world that is digitally and globally connected and highly networked. Creating high-performing virtual teams is the order of the day, a need of the hour.

The cost of travel, the time associated with travel, and the speed with which business needs to be conducted are some of the factors we need to take into account. These can be some of the constraints faced by people in conducting their businesses, but as it is said, "change begins at the end of one's comfort zone." The pandemic, in its own way, has succeeded in disrupting much of our comfort zones and has now ensured that teams can be both virtual as well as physical.

However, the emphasis is now on virtual teams and the skills required for managing virtual teams. This can be a little different from the way one manages a physical team. Both kinds of teams have their own merits and demerits, like the two sides of a coin. But the fact remains that the world is going to be a hub of networking and digitalization. On the same note, managing virtual teams is going to be a very important skill that managers will have to develop.

This is particularly relevant for those managers who hitherto operated in very traditional ways: physically meeting people, engaging over cups of tea and coffee, having social engagements, and conducting social events. Things now need to be done in a different way.

> *"It isn't enough to think outside the box. Thinking is passive. Get used to acting outside the box."* —Tim Ferriss.

As the quote infers, managers now need to reinvent themselves and change their way of thinking; they need to add the required skills to their kitty in terms of managing high-performing virtual teams.

To manage and lead high-performing virtual teams, one needs to look at these questions: How does one set goals with virtual teams? What are some of the key challenges associated with it? How do you keep teams engaged? How to keep teams motivated? How do you have commonly shared goals which are communicated with impact? How do you assess the performance of virtual teams? How can you coach, give feedback, and develop the team? And how do you ensure collaboration and trust in teams virtually? These are some of the key challenges which managers face. Although they might seem like a lot of questions, they are all pertinent.

However, as the saying goes, 'stronger the setback, the stronger is the comeback.' Therefore, in this chapter, we will learn how to deal effectively with virtual teams and have a more globally connected world even during bad times.

We all would agree that empathy is a hallmark of civilization. It can be described more poetically as seeing with the eyes of another, listening through loaned ears, and feeling through a different heart. But when it comes to virtual teams, the first challenge is how we form this sort of connection online. How do you connect with people virtually? How do you ensure teams remain connected? How do you set the right kind of goals and standards? Video conferencing is an efficacious tool for engaging with teams today. It is a cost-effective option where all you need is a good internet connection. There are facilities like breakout rooms, where one can connect with a smaller group to put across your presentations and receive feedback from the people. In fact, global events are now being conducted virtually. The digital landscape and technology have helped us get connected, and it is as good as people seeing each other.

Therefore, in setting performance goals in a virtual team, the parameters you need to consider are the quality of work produced and the speed at which it is completed, rather than the hours put in by a person. Performance goals in virtual teams have to be very specific, measurable, attainable, relevant, and time-bound.

One must remember when setting these goals that all interactions have to be managed virtually, and goals necessarily dependent on physical interactions have to be avoided.

These goals invariably focus on flexibility and agility. Setting the standards for a virtual team is very similar to the way we would set goals if it were done face to face for a physical team, which again is not an easy task.

In virtual teams, there is increased flexibility in terms of how people work and where they work from. However, these are very crucial elements for a virtual team. The team members could be working from home, or they could be working out of a coffee shop. What is important is that they deliver the results and reach their goals on time, and they do it keeping the specifications and the quality intact. It is also important to ensure that those working in roles that require a lot of data privacy and data confidentiality are able to maintain those norms. In short, efficiency should be measured in terms of output, quality, and speed, rather than where they work from. These are some of the key parameters which one needs to consider while setting performance goals for virtual teams.

Good communication demarcates confusion and clarity. Hence, the next important area to focus on is communicating the set performance goals to the virtual team; this can be done through virtual video conferencing. The set goals, the process to be followed to achieve them, and the steps that need to be taken can be shared virtually in a very effective manner. Without proper evaluation, failure is inevitable. So naturally, the next thing we should do is look for a way of evaluating these goals. Evaluation of goals has to be purely on qualitative parameters like the flexibility in attending meetings and taking the initiative in the meetings.

As for the other regular competencies which we would normally evaluate, it is taken that what team members demonstrate face-to-face and what they demonstrate virtually will be quite similar. However, ensuring team engagement in virtual teams is quite important. And with regard to managers in virtual teams, they ought to be easily available to the team members and also more approachable. Managers should try to have as much video talk time as possible with their team, which is the new normal for face-to-face interactions, and it is very effective as well. Of course, being available in this context refers to meeting virtually rather than waiting for a face-to-face meeting.

Moreover, it is important to set the performance goals quickly, and the team should be encouraged to begin executing these performance goals immediately, rather than waiting for a physical meeting. The above mentioned are the important skills needed for virtual team leadership. In my experience, setting goals for a virtual team by meeting the members through a virtual medium is not that different from setting goals while interacting with people face to face.

The only additional comfort factor is when you meet somebody physically, there is more informal social interaction, you can have a cup of tea or coffee together, and you probably will bond a little more. But apart from that, the quality of work does not change. When one is working digitally, and especially when one is making video calls, all we have to do is adapt to the new normal. This is just like how now we pick our keys and wallet while going out, but do not forget the new addition to this, our masks.

People everywhere need motivation at some point in their lives. A little push is something all of us would welcome and want at times because a completely virtual work schedule can be exhausting. Motivating a virtual team requires the same energy and dedication as it does for a physical team. Maybe even a little more than what it takes for a physical team. For effective interaction with the team, you need to keep two things in focus: the quality of interaction and the frequency of interaction. I have coached clients whom I have never met in person. That has not changed the relationship or had any impact on the quality of inputs that I have been able to give them. It is all about getting into that level of comfort in the pandemic situation. The question initially was, where do you find new clients? Where do you find senior executives? I have not even met my clients face to face in many cases.

Earlier, 98 percent of my work interactions were face-to-face, and 2 percent took place virtually. Post-pandemic, for a period of 12 months, 100 percent of my work happened virtually, but that does not mean that the quality of interaction or the quality of inputs has changed. Yes, I would have loved to meet and interact with my clients over a cup of coffee. But one should be able to build a relationship irrespective of the situation, and any thoughts to the contrary are merely mind blocks. It is all about being able to handle things in the new normal. We need to get comfortable with the new situation by addressing the issues in our minds.

Therefore, as I mentioned earlier, a successful virtual team involves the accessibility of the leader when the team needs them and the accessibility of the team members when the leader needs to interact with them. There are multiple digital platforms available that you can use to connect with your team virtually. However, there is also a need to assess performance.

I can personally vouch for virtualization and virtual teamwork as it was in the first eight to ten months of virtual handling, our coaching business grew multifold. In the virtual world, I could handle a greater number of clients in a day than I could when I was interacting face to face.

So, my productivity increased dramatically. I got more out of my working hours than I did when I was physically interacting in person with my clients because face-to-face physical interactions consume a significant amount of travel time, which was unproductive time.

For example, for a two- or a four-hour coaching session, I used to spend a day in travel. Today, the same four hours are effectively used, and I work nine hours a day.

My productivity has drastically increased by more than 100 percent. The digital platforms today offer a number of facilities, like breakout rooms, sharing of PowerPoint presentations, sharing of presentations on the screen and interacting with the client, and sharing feedback. People can show up on the screen and share anything they want. There is no radical change involved, except that one has to be open to the change and accept it. For development, a lot of common classroom training can be done virtually. One of the challenges to be considered here is that it may not be possible to see all the participants simultaneously, especially when you have a group interaction.

That is not necessarily a challenge, but it definitely needs a little bit of getting used to. Looking at your audience while delivering a lecture or a presentation is usually recommended. This aids you in forming a personal connection and also enables you to assess their reactions and responses and improvise then and there as necessary. But when it comes to virtual meetings, these things become nonexistent. Many times, one has to prompt the participants to get a response. The maturity level of the participants and their commitment toward learning and development is of paramount importance. If the participant is involved as much as you are, you can always expect a response.

The same is also relevant in a classroom, except that the classroom facilitator can generate more interactions. There are slightly more interactions in a classroom than in a virtual meeting. One could generate interaction in a virtual meeting by asking questions or even starting off with an icebreaker activity and taking a pause every five to seven minutes to check the progress. Or you can restructure your group activities in such a way that every five to seven minutes, the group has to pivot for a 10-minute exercise.

This is workable and recommended because the attention span of the participants is around seven to ten minutes in the virtual world, and their attention will reduce significantly beyond 10 minutes. This is how it works, and no one is to blame.

It is of note that the number of distractions is markedly high when one is working from home. The reasons for this include the fact that people may not have a quiet space to work from, or there may be personal distractions like mobile phones and social media platforms. It is also physically very challenging to work from your bed, which is where most people go wrong. Working on your bed makes you feel lethargic, and it is almost impossible not to fall asleep or sulk. It is a demotivating habit. Creating a small workstation in your own room or in any corner of the house can help greatly. This helps sustain discipline during work hours. The concept of home offices has risen over the pandemic.

However, distractions are a part of life, whether it is offline or online. So, one just needs to factor in the same. In short, with virtual teams, the quality of interaction has not changed, the content has not changed, and even 25 percent of delivery has not changed; what has changed is that every 10 minutes, you have a group activity. When it is offline, you would usually initiate a group activity after 45 minutes or one hour. There is no difference in the delivery of the core content or message.

It is all in the perception. Developing high-performing teams can be done digitally well enough. We have, of course, heard of virtual learning methods. The number of self-taught leaders, entrepreneurs, and artists is multiplying every day. In fact, self-taught individuals have a larger scale of success. The eLearning courses and platforms play a huge part in this. Because:

- E-Learning packages offer people a chance to learn at their own convenience through video recorded messages, which happens to be a very good way of developing virtual teams.
- Coaching can happen quicker and faster with more flexibility as compared to waiting for face-to-face interaction.
- Since eLearning is mostly self-paced, it demands the individual to bring in enough discipline to make it through the course.
- eLearning is a great way to gain access to resources, coaches, and leaders from all across the world while sitting in your own room. Resources that were previously unattainable due to distance can now be easily accessed through these courses.
- The peer mentor or the buddy system is another very effective way of developing virtual teams and connecting with each other.
- Virtual training and eLearning enable many people having the same interests to connect together on a platform, which opens discussions.

This can indeed be a great tool to learn better and explore different perspectives.
- In summary, training, coaching, and counseling on a virtual platform can help build virtual teams, and buddy mentoring can also aid in developing virtual meetings.

CASE STUDY:

Let us consider how virtual teams have had an impact. Case studies can help a group of learners or others to focus on a specific concept or help them solve a problem. Let us consider the example of a technology firm that had to undergo a major transition and reinvent itself during the pandemic phase. The organization was partly used to virtual working through live sessions and conferencing, which accounted for about 10% to 15% of the work. The rest 85% was done face to face by meeting people, traveling, interacting with clients, and interacting with team members.

So, from an 85% offline and 15% virtual model, the company needed to transition to a major virtual working model. The pandemic situation has substantially changed the necessities of the organization. During this time, there were major disruptions because of imposed lockdown and changes in the business environment of the European, American, Canadian, and Australian markets, which contributed to 60% of their revenues, and the Asian market, which contributed 40% of their revenues. The organization had to go through a major change in strategy to reduce the risk from the 60% dependency and also focus on emerging markets like Asia and Africa. To focus on these markets, they also had to hire a new workforce.

They also had to prospect organizations that they could acquire, and all of this was done virtually through video conferencing. We have also seen the example of Reliance and Facebook investing in Reliance, which was accomplished virtually. Hence, a business can be transacted virtually without the comfort and necessity of meeting people face to face. In reference to this particular case study, the organization has transitioned from being a traditional software development company to one that develops digital technology that can be used to drive a business.

It has now introduced new digital products and has changed its strategy from focusing on the traditional sectors, that is, the traditional markets of the US, Canada, and Europe. It has now shifted its focus to Australia and Asia. This has also meant acquiring new companies, which was done online.

So how did this happen? Leveraging digital technology platforms and goal setting was done as usual, but it happened virtually. Regular periodic online meetings were taking place virtually every week. We ensured that the managers were accessible to the team when needed. They were getting real-time information about the employees—not only about their performance but also their personal lives, that is, the wellness of their families. For the teams who were in India when the second wave of the pandemic hit, the organization was able to be of help. The entire workspace was converted into a Covid care center for their teams and their families. They also contributed to setting up ventilator support in various centers in India. Notably, the contributions were not large-scale Covid facilities but small-scale facilities of 20-25 beds. But every little drop of water contributes to forming the ocean, and progression is progression no matter how small. Beds that were unutilized were also made available to the public, although the employees and their families were given priority. During Covid times, they even made a contribution to the society as a part of the CSR (Corporate Social Responsibility) Fund, and contributed to the Prime Minister's Fund and the Chief Minister's Fund, and also to other charitable social causes. It is interesting to note that the organization registered double-digit growth during these difficult times. Pre-pandemic, the employees were accustomed to 85% travel, but now, they were all working virtually without wasting any time on travel. This translated to more productivity in less time. The organization is planning to resume work from the office only in April of 2022.

So, for more than one and a half years, almost close to two years, the organization has driven growth and profitability virtually. It has hired people and has continued to invest in people's development and training through virtual online programs and virtual coaching programs for senior leaders. It is an honor to say that I have been one of the coaches as well. Their revenues have grown; they have also completed the acquisition of companies. All of this was achieved without physically meeting anybody. They did everything right, at the right time.

They maintained a high level of engagement and focused on wellness; they undertook wellness initiatives for not only the employees but also their families. At the same time, they have also contributed to society at large by not only making donations to the CSR fund but also leveraging and outsourcing some of their spare facilities and offices as part-time Covid care facilities. This goes to show that teams can be built virtually.

I can testify that video conferencing is a very effective way of delivering business performance; all you need is a good internet connection, a clear screen, and uninterrupted time. In fact, a lot of teams have also mentioned that their performance has gone up by working virtually because that has eliminated a lot of unproductive time—watercooler discussions and tea breaks. Working virtually also helps people manage their time more efficiently and enables them to take time out for their personal development. A number of people have mentioned that instead of spending one or two days completely away from work for training, it has now been spread over four or five days with two hours a day devoted to training. The employees have found this schedule to be far more engaging. People have been able to concentrate much more in a two-hour session than they did in a full-day classroom training session.

The market is continually adapting to 'The New Normal,' and one of those changes is the use of online meeting platforms. The Covid-19 outbreak has created a new space for video conferencing and potentially changed the way people will communicate going forward. In the span of a few months, video chat has gone from a futuristic way of keeping in touch to an essential part of our daily lives. A recent article mentioned this, saying, "Many of the first companies to build modern video communication systems as we know them were tech pioneers who saw the impact that video conferencing could have across business and personal lives alike. But when cloud computing hit the scene, any company that could develop an easy-to-use tool with a good interface had just as much of a shot of being successful in the space." In 2020, there was a huge range of video communication platforms to choose from based on your needs. Some video tech providers have had more 'use cases' with the public over the years. Social media platforms have incorporated video into their messaging apps so that you can talk face to face with the click of a button. Other video tech systems, like Cisco's WebEx and the now mega-popular Zoom, were mainly used by businesses to streamline communication with customers and teams in different locations.

Now, they are getting a lot more traffic.

We know that the education system is evolving faster than ever and it has been impacted fiercely by the pandemic. An article by world economic forum states "While countries are at different points in their COVID-19 infection rates, worldwide there are currently more than 1.2 billion children in 186 countries affected by school closures due to the pandemic.

In Denmark, children up to the age of 11 are returning to nurseries and schools after initially closing on 12 March, but in South Korea students are responding to roll calls from their teachers online. Many are curious about the future of learning mechanisms. Will online teaching continue to persist post-pandemic? How will it impact the education industry? Even before Covid-19, there was already high growth and adoption in education technology, with global EdTech investments reaching US$ 18.66 billion in 2019, and the overall market for online education was projected to reach $350 billion by 2025.

Whether it is language apps, virtual tutoring, video conferencing tools, or online learning software, there has been a significant surge in usage since COVID-19. Overall, we can say that virtual teams have proven to be more advantageous than a limitation. We have to adapt ourselves to change and make the best of the situation. Above all, we have to realize that human touch, sympathy, and empathy form the essence of life, and without these, there is always emptiness. This feeling needs to be addressed and the gap bridged.

But given the situation, how best do we overcome the obstacle? It is by these virtual connections that we can make and bridge gaps in the best way possible. The hybrid model will be the rule of the day. Hybrid models, both offline and online methods of developing teams, will continue to drive profitability and sustainability in the future.

We would do well to embrace it.

The final key message which I would like to leave with you is in the context of managing virtual teams. I think authenticity, consistency, clarity, and speed of response are the four key deliverables which go a long way in ensuring relationships are maintained and sustained.

TAKEAWAYS:

- Change is needed, they say, but we also have to realize that change is inevitable. The pandemic was a realization of the same. The world is changing, and the business world is not an exception. If digitalization allows for more of a globally connected world, why not?
- Virtual teams may be challenging at first in terms of good internet connections, lack of discipline from the individual's end, low attention levels, and more.

But it is also true that virtualization has been a game-changer for many companies over the pandemic.

- This is the reason why it must be explored fully. Many high-performing virtual teams have pulled up their socks and started working again. Numerous small businesses flourished online. I have personally felt a drastic change in business as I was able to devote more time to clients virtually than I did by traveling for hours to meet them.
- Video conferencing also helps in checking in on your people to find out if they are fine and alright. It is as good as seeing a person face to face, other than the psychological comfort of meeting a person.
- As mentioned in the case study, digitalization did not make an organization any less human. The company not only successfully acquired smaller companies and increased their workforce, but it also contributed back to society.
- Digitalization has proven to be more cost-efficient, with the added advantage of a global talent pool.
- eLearning is a vital part of developing virtual teams. It provides access to well-polished courses from around the globe anywhere, anytime.
- Virtual teams allow for discussion among different teams, which in a way enables mentoring and a buddy system. Many perspectives come together, and from them, many ideas. This has also promoted a healthier and more productive lifestyle for the employees.

14

MANAGING DIVERSITY AND INCLUSION

"What divides us pales in comparison to what unites us.
- Edward Kennedy

There are just five minutes left for your work hours to start, you have an important meeting today, and you are rushing against all odds to reach the office on time. You finally arrive huffing and puffing to find the smiling faces of your colleagues. You notice, not for the first time, that your team is made up of people from different age groups, nationalities, colors, cultural backgrounds, and genders. Yet, it amazes you every time.

There is a meeting scheduled for later in the day. You have so many ideas to express. You are not very much sure about some of them, but you do not have to worry about it much. You know your team is compassionate enough to help you out. The meeting goes well. You hear many voices; there was constructive feedback, and ideas were exchanged with each other. There were some points that have been disagreed upon respectfully, but that will be looked into later. You come out of the meeting room with satisfaction written on your face and go to the cafeteria where you meet your friends from the same building and spend some time. No one feels left out.

In the evening, you leave the building exhausted due to the day's work but with a sense of contentment. And you silently thank your stars for being placed in such an institution. This would be the scenario of a normal working day for a person working in an organization that has diversity and inclusion.

Diversity in the workplace implies that an organization employs a workforce that includes a wide range of people from different genders, age groups, religions, cultural backgrounds, ethnicity, origins, and educational qualifications, and they may differ in many more aspects. Diversity in the workforce contributes toward a plethora of benefits like new perspectives, a wider talent pool, more innovation, better employee performance, and increased performance.

It was mentioned in the website Science Daily that "Companies reporting the highest levels of racial diversity brought in nearly 15 times more sales revenue on average than those with the lowest levels of racial diversity." A good example of this is Accenture PLC, which was ranked as the top, diverse organization by Thomson Reuters 2018 Diversity and Inclusion Index.

It is not enough to just have diversity in the workforce. It is also important that each one feels included in the team. This is where the term inclusion comes in. When an employee is given the space to thrive, it is known as inclusion. It can also be considered as the voice of diversity.

With great inclusion, there is great employee engagement. According to the Peakon Post website, inclusion gives a 6.2% increase in on-the-job effort, a 5% increase in employees' intent to stay, and a nearly 3% increase in individual employee performance. The eight components of inclusion are having a voice, feeling of belonging, sense of uniqueness, feeling valued, learning and development, collaborative environment, access to resources, and strategic alignment.

"We are all different, which is great because we are all unique. Without diversity, life would be very boring," said Catherine Pulsifer. True to her words, we have an estimated population of 7.9 billion in this world and approximately 1.38 billion people in India alone, with an expansive range of cultural and demographic attributes. Just as an Islamic proverb states, "A lot of different flowers make a bouquet," a firm needs diverse employees to bring out the optimum results. This is diversity and inclusion.

Diversity and inclusion are complementary and synergistic words that drive a culture of high performance as well as innovation in any organization, be it a business, political, or social organization.

But the essence of diversity is not always maintained in every workplace. The essence has been lost in a few places. Unfortunately, a number of organizations are just looking at diversity for adding numbers to the game. Either they are looking at gender diversity in isolation, or they are looking at the LGBTQ community to score a few brownie points. The truth is, diversity goes way beyond that. Diversity and inclusion are based on the concept of meritocracy. It is the right person for the right role, irrespective of age, caste, creed, religion, gender, and sexual orientation of an individual. Nowadays, a quota is a common term.

Each organization, including educational firms, has reservations at various levels for minorities or for those belonging to a particular caste, religion, gender, or any other group of people. Sadly, one fails to understand that when one introduces the "quota system," one is actually moving away from the concept of meritocracy. Meritocracy means giving the right people the right to opportunity, and it is not just about hiring and considering the numbers, which is the dominant scenario in the global environment.

One such situation is where the regulation requires firms to include a certain number of women in the workforce; we see a few women added as independent directors in the Indian context. Arlan Hamilton said, "If you haven't hired a team of people who are of color, female, or LGBT to turn over every stone actively, to scope out every nook and cranny, to pop out of every bush, to find every qualified underrepresented founder in this country, you're going to miss out on a lot of money when the rest of the investment world gets it." It is a good concept to initiate diverse people into the workforce, but the selection has to be done the right way for it to work out.

In many organizations where I have worked in the past, I have noticed a lot of resistance to women who returned to their jobs after taking a career break. I have also seen situations where the HR teams would try to fill in the numbers and not necessarily hire the right people for the right job. Line managers frequently complain that we are getting into a quota system and are moving away from the concept of meritocracy. These are some of the real challenges that we need to address. A considerable number of women who are hired are returning either from a maternity break or a long career break, and it is important that the right environment be created for them to succeed. We need to adopt policies that allow for flexible working hours or include part-time options. It is also imperative that managers undergo sensitivity training to ensure the safety and security of women.

If we are hiring from the LGBTQ community, we should ensure that they are treated on par. The right kind of infrastructure has to be ensured, and they should be made to feel included in the team. They should be included in terms of the different ways they can add to the team and the different skills they bring to the table. And when it comes to making critical and important decisions, their views should be heard.

A great example is Tim Cook, CEO of Apple. He was appointed as CEO in 2011, and in 2013, he sent a memo to his employees stating that Apple supported federal government protections against LGBTQ discrimination. Diversity and inclusion cannot be driven by regulation; instead, they can be driven through social awareness and through a sense of ownership by the leaders, complemented with training both for managers and leaders as well as for the people being inducted into the workforce.

In terms of workplace infrastructure, the environment should be conducive, and proper hygiene facilities should be in place. Crèches must be made available where working mothers or single parents can leave their children safe even if they have to work for extended hours. So, one needs to really offer the right kind of infrastructural support to enable diversity and inclusion to flourish and succeed.

Very often, people do not have a diversity and inclusion strategy in place. In my corporate career, the organizations I was with have been recognized and rewarded for the various steps they have undertaken in diversity inclusion. I have been an advocate for that. The starting point of diversity and inclusion has a clear strategy in place.

What are we really looking at? How do we develop and focus on this module called DARE—Develop, Attract, Retain, and Engage?

Having a clear strategy to develop, attract, retain, and engage talent is the basis of meritocracy and not really a quota system. When one is setting a strategy to develop people, what kind of training should be given? First, we need to balance technical, functional, soft skills, and sensitivity training to people. To attract talent, one needs to have the right kind of work environment, the right kind of work culture, the right kind of support system, and the right kind of career growth opportunity. Quoting Nellie Borrero, "Diversity is a fact, but inclusion is a choice we make every day.

As leaders, we have to put out the message that we embrace and not just tolerate diversity." For this, one should ensure that people are not at a disadvantage.

Many women who return to the workplace after taking a break for personal reasons are not compensated adequately despite having the requisite skills and qualifications. In my opinion, one of the worst ways to treat a person is by not compensating them according to their merit. Next, one needs to ensure that gender disparity in compensation is neutralized because eventually if a person is found capable of doing a job, they should not be short-changed just because they are of a different gender or they come from a different ethnic or cultural background. They should be treated on merit. There needs to be the right kind of compensation framework. Pay for performance and pay for capability. This should be the guiding force to attract talent as well. To retain talent, as mentioned before, we need the right kind of policies, the right kind of ecosystems, and the right kind of support from the managers of the organization. And we need to have career paths.

Last but not least, we need to ensure adequate compensation. When we engage people, we need to make them inclusive as a part of the workforce. Do not promote people just because there is a quota system that has to be filled, but promote people on merit. When people on merit are being promoted, they become role models for others to follow. After all, who does not want to be a role model for people to follow?

I have worked with male managers and female managers in the past. Also, I coach male and female leaders as well. I have observed that capability is beyond gender: be it a man or a woman, if they are capable, nothing can come in their way of achieving success. We need to address these challenges in our minds. Another challenge I have come across while working in global organizations is ethnicity. Since I was from a very different ethnic background, I was not treated on par with others and faced hurdles in my career. I had the qualifications and the capability, but some people were adamant about not giving me the right opportunities. So instead of playing the role of a victim, the key here is you need to work that extra little bit harder. Eventually, people will acknowledge the strengths you bring to the table. So, my advice would be, even if at times you face challenges at the workplace because of your ethnicity, gender, or sexual orientation, bring it to the attention of the right people. Work that little extra bit harder.

Do not let yourself feel like a victim, and do not play the victim. If you have the capability, nobody can deny things for too long. Eventually, you are going to get there. Remember, truth does prevail. Justice may be slightly delayed, but it will never be denied.

There are several instances where people have gone beyond their minority status and have been successful in all walks of life. Maritime capability should be the key driving point. After all, as Jesse Jackson says, "when everyone is included, everyone wins." When people are included, they have a sense of belonging, which makes them feel that their workplace is their second home. And everyone wants the best for their homes; hence, this results in maximum positive outcomes.

When discussing diversity, the other area that has to be highlighted is bringing in different perspectives. This is where people and leaders come in, especially when they have people with different views of their own. Different views are actually a strength. Because different views help you think differently, they help you look at the coin from two perspectives. Otherwise, you will end up seeing the point from a singular perspective and sometimes do so with blinkers in your eyes.

To drive innovation, you need different thought processes. You need somebody to challenge the status quo. Sometimes, you also need an external person to show you the mirror, whether it is a coach, a colleague, or a member of your family—basically, somebody who can be honest with us and hold up the mirror. The ability of people to accept honest feedback is the hallmark of achieving high performance.

Hence, for building high-performing teams, diversity and inclusion are important ingredients. Adding to the same, stereotypical people in a team will not drive high growth; instead, it will drive only incremental growth. Diversity has to be holistic.

Consider the case of diversity in education: having a bunch of people with similar educational backgrounds from similar institutes will never encourage diversity. People of different genders should also be included to have the right balance here because different people think differently. People should be given a fair opportunity based on their merit rather than only having a policy in place and inducting people just to show and get awards. The policies must be followed in principle, and in addition to a fair opportunity, everyone should be given equal status in the group. Respect people for what they are, rather than for how they look, how they behave, or how they are oriented.

A crucial element in terms of diversity and inclusion relating to high-performing teams is to ensure that a leader has the right maturity to understand the strengths of each individual and build a culture of trust, mutual respect, and collaboration within the team.

That is where the leader plays a very important role not only for the organization but also in making every individual feel included. If people do not feel valued and respected or they do not have a feeling of security, high-performing teams cannot be created, and the concept will not work. This does not suggest that underperformance can be tolerated. But one cannot live with a sword hanging over your neck all the time. Therefore, this is another area where a lot of work has to be done.

A survey by Globalization Partners Inc. stated that 9 out of 10 people had described their company to be diverse, but 3 out of 10 reported that inclusion was not present. Where do organizations go wrong in diversity and inclusion? What are some of the challenges they face, and what should organizations do to build a culture of diversity and inclusion? I would say it begins with the wrong requisition process.

As mentioned previously, there is no clear strategy, and organizations look at diversity purely in isolation. They usually have a policy for diversity and inclusion, which is isolated and not linked to the entire objective of the organization. Second, the policy will not really define what they mean by diversity, or they try to restrict diversity to gender diversity hiring. But diversity goes beyond that. Third, they look at diversity in terms of an isolated policy, for example, an LGBTQ policy that comes in to create an award for diversity. But inclusion is less about chasing awards and more about driving high performance and innovation. It is creating a culture of trust, collaboration, and mutual respect. Many organizations move away from inclusion. The other area where organizations are unable to implement inclusion in the right way is in providing the correct infrastructure; for example, differently-abled people should have the right kind of washrooms with the proper railings.

An organization can have the best policies, but if they do not provide the basic conveniences, they will face difficulties in keeping people engaged. The cafeterias should be friendly for differently-abled people. One may need unisex washrooms in certain situations, especially for the transgender community, who may find it uncomfortable to use either the male or the female washrooms.

One needs to get into those details that organizations usually miss out on in the meetings. When organizations hire people, it is also their responsibility to make them comfortable and provide the right facilities and basic conveniences.

In December 2020, Infosys launched a practice guideline that aimed to provide a better environment for the differently-abled by enabling, informing, and sensitizing functions in the workforce, which received tremendous support.

Such initiatives will make the differently-abled people feel included and allow them a fair chance to come out and contribute. There will not be any setbacks. It is the organization's responsibility to ensure that there are no setbacks. It is crucial to have the right set of managers supporting their people. It should not matter whether they hired somebody who is returning from maternity leave or somebody who is returning from a long sabbatical. One needs to be sensitive and encouraging enough to integrate them into the deal. Managers need to be sensitized toward handling diversity: diversity in thoughts, diversity in profiles, diversity in skills, and diversity in genders. Therefore, all managers need to be trained for this. A culture of trust and collaboration has to be built, which can happen both formally and informally and should be reflected in daily actions.

It is seen that all leaders virtually talk about it in seminars, but they do not necessarily walk their talk when it comes down to action. The initiation of this process is by training. Training is not a one-time activity where you hire a consultant, and they train you on what diversity is in the form of a workshop and go back at the end of the day. Training has to be done on a regular basis. Diversity and inclusion training should not be only limited to training on PoSH (Prevention of Sexual Harassment) but must go well beyond that. It has to be a regular culture. And that culture has to be linked in terms of the basis of hiring people, the way a person should be treated, how a person should be rewarded, and the various kinds of career opportunities that will be created for them.

There was a wonderful organization that I was consulting with. I was quite impressed with the technology of the company. I was impressed with the way they dealt with the team. The team consisted of people with different profiles and different nationalities. That is another important part. If you get too focused on only one particular nationality in a team, it is not driving diversity. This was a team where nobody looked alike, for there were people with different nationalities and genders: it was a wonderful sight.

I did not want to consciously count people because then you get into the numbers game and that numbers game is absolutely an incorrect way of measuring diversity.

That is the part where many companies get it wrong; they get into the numbers game, calculating the percentage of women in the workforce, percentage of LBGTQ persons, percentage of differently-abled people, and so on. The more an organization gets into the numbers game, the more they are moving away from the essence of a culture of diversity. At the end of the day, culture is the most important measure, and it is reflected in performance. This is called cultural performance.

As I have mentioned over and over, the key to good training is consistency. In reference to the organization I previously mentioned, though people were of different backgrounds, during the discussions, the team members were respectful to each other. They understood each other's strengths and challenged each other constructively. Naturally, one can expect a lot of debate when challenged constructively. They were able to bring forward different views. But in the end, they agreed to a point, and in areas where they did not agree, they agreed to disagree and moved on to implement the idea as if it was their own. This was beautiful to experience, as it was only the beginning of a high-performing team. All the points on the checklist were met.

This means that they had people from different backgrounds, including educational backgrounds, nationalities, different genders, and thought processes, but eventually, they had an environment of trust and were willing to challenge each other; they were willing to collaborate with each other and were willing to agree to disagree. The most successful organizations in this world use diversity and inclusion as the keys to success. One such example is the Alibaba group. In 2017, the transactions on its clothing sites summed up to 248 billion dollars. Jack Ma, the head of Alibaba, describes women as the "secret sauce" for this success. He claimed that "women's perseverance and attention to details will outperform men in the age of robotics and machine learning."

Another example of this is Accenture, as mentioned earlier. It has paired up with more than three-quarters of the Global Fortune 500 companies and is spread across 120 countries. They state that diversity at the workplace is at the core of their success. Forbes's top multinational performer L'Oreal is another great example. Women form 69 percent of their workforce, and they are known to sponsor disability workshops in India. They also pair their employees with multicultural students of the Netherlands and also provide training to vulnerable adult Pakistan communities.

The world's largest PC vendor Lenovo received a perfect score of 100 on the Corporate Equality Index for LGBTQ equality. Yolanda Conyers, the company's chief diversity officer, states that "serving a global customer base requires more than out-of-the-box thinking because it's not just one box. It is a hundred different boxes or a million different boxes. It takes every dimension of our diversity. All our diverse mindsets, skills, and cultural backgrounds, to deliver such a wide array of technology." Uber, one of the popular cab services, has taken the initiative to recognize and eliminate sexism to create a safe workplace. Banana Republic has chosen to teach its employees to celebrate cultural differences.

These companies can be role models for other companies and can provide a base for the ideas that will induce the movement of diversity and inclusion in the organizations.

TAKEAWAYS:

- Do not look at diversity as a numbers game; look at creating an environment of hiring the right people for the right job. After hiring, focus on developing them into a team. Post that, your main focus should be on ensuring that everything is in place to have them retained. Check consistently if they are being engaged really well.
- Create a culture that has respect, security, trust, and collaboration. People should value each other and should be comfortable in challenging the status quo. They should be able to freely bring in new ideas without creating an environment of insecurity or penalizing. A supportive and warm environment goes a long way. This can be possible only from a good selection process, as mentioned in the previous point.
- Have a clear strategy in place. What is it that you want to achieve? What is your mission? What is your vision? What is the purpose of your strategy? It is important to relate to that strategy in a holistic way rather than looking at it in pillars of isolation.
- Another major point is to create the right kind of enablers and infrastructure. If the workplace does not have those, then the workers will not be completely satisfied, and this will not give hundred percent results. This will be an overall loss for the company.
- A satisfied and content employee brings the best for the firm.

That satisfaction can be brought only through the right kind of environment that enables the culture of diversity and inclusion.

- Another important point to note is that you should continue to invest regularly, periodically, and consistently in training and development. Diversity and inclusion are things that cannot be achieved with just one training session in the beginning. These pieces of training should include activities that will help people to learn about each other's cultures and gain a higher set of knowledge. This has proven to have worked in the overall development of the organization.

15

CREATING A CULTURE OF HIGH PERFORMANCE

"Culture is the process by which a person becomes all that they were created capable of being."

-Thomas Carlyle

We hear the word culture very often in our lives. Culture is the term that encompasses the social behavior and norms followed by our societies. It is inclusive of the knowledge, beliefs, customs, capabilities, and habits of the individuals in the social group. The habits that we see practiced around us have a huge influence on the sort of culture we develop. As babies, we observe the language spoken by those around us, and we learn to speak it as well, without anybody really trying hard to teach us. The same holds true for culture also. It is a collection of different habits and practices that have influenced us and continue to inspire us to grow. A cultural norm defines acceptable conduct in society; it certainly serves as a guideline of how we conduct ourselves in the community.

In the United Kingdom, scholars influenced by people like Stuart Hall and Raymond Williams developed cultural studies.

Following the prevalent habits, they identified "culture" with consumer goods and leisure activities such as art, music, film, food, sports, and clothing. It is an essential feature to incorporate cultural habits into whatever we do. It surely changes the rhythm and lays down the field for work.

When it comes to building high-performing teams, what are the interesting cultural features that we can incorporate? Culture is the root of every aspect, even for a high-performing team. Allow me to begin by addressing what causes a high-performance culture and what goes into driving a high-performance culture. Let us define what we mean by high-performance culture. A high-performance culture is creating the right environment, the right type of enablers, and a culture of trust, collaboration, and recognition for surpassing normal expected standards and recognition for going beyond the normal routine. People go to work with a clear mindset of growing and developing.

High performance begins with the heart and then gets converted into skills and subsequently to vision. Culture plays a very important role in building high-performing teams, and it is a very important ingredient in determining a team's success. The culture of high performance includes three important elements:

- First, it is the ability to check if the teams have the right knowledge and skills to do the job.
- Second, do they have the right enablers? Do they have the right information they need? Do they have the right tools? Do they have the right technology? Do they have the right processes?
- And third, are they abiding by the culture?

People look forward to resolving challenges that come with their jobs to get to a better position. But people appreciate this process only when they have proper guidance and mentors.

Therefore, it is the responsibility of the mentor to build a high-performing team and drive team members to the next level of performance. The responsibility of a mentor is crucial, and their guidance is definitely needed for a person's betterment. This engagement will lead to a high-performance culture and hence the overall growth of the team. However, the process is not an easy one.

There are many challenges that have to be faced. One of the major challenges would be task management.

Although it may seem obvious, leaders who mismanage tasks within their team environment risk disrupting its balance. Individuals and the group will work best depending on what motivates them to do better: variety, task importance, or feedback. Engagement is a major challenge. There is a definite connection between the performance of individuals within a team and the level to which they feel engaged. Leaders who attain a high understanding of employee empowerment skills can best empower their people and create the ownership that helps productivity. These skills include communication, emotional intelligence, influencing and listening skills, and negotiation skills.

Conflict resolution and organizational issues come next. Conflict is a naturally occurring event within any group. It can either be constructive or destructive. Leaders who take a concerted approach rather than a confronting approach in their communicative technique will encourage open communication. The organizational structure will impact a team's effectiveness. How team members interact with others, the support they receive from their seniors, and the resources available will all be predominant factors in their performance.

Overall, the leader should be able to guide his teammates through the team's goals. Most importantly, they should be able to visualize where the team member will fit best in the arena of responsibility, and they should be aware of how their performance will contribute to the overall growth. When everyone in the team has a clear picture of their roles and responsibilities, they are motivated to work harder.

Overcoming team leadership challenges allows for the creation of an effective team, which will produce the following benefits:

- Employees show creativity in problem-solving.
- Once all the concerned personnel understands their job, employers can retain them, and it reduces a significant amount of cost.
- Better time management comes into the picture.

So, what should we do to create a culture of high performance? Let us consider some of the foundational elements and key procedures that would accelerate the chances of creating a high-performing team. I have surveyed more than 150 organizations, covering multinational corporations, law sectors, large Indian global corporations, family-run businesses, and some public sector undertakings.

It has helped me to understand what contributes to a culture of high performance. For example, if a business grows at 10% per annum, achieving a 10% growth is not something that is extraordinary. But yes, growing 100%, when the industry grows at 10% that would be an important ingredient in over-riding high performance. Of course, one way to do that depends on the state of the organization and the correct pace level. A start-up will have a faster growth rate; mature organizations will have a slower growth rate.

A significant element is about driving a culture of innovation. So, creating a culture of high performance essentially requires that we practice innovation and keep raising the bar enough to challenge people to grow beyond the stipulated industry growth rates. Innovation is a very important factor: what new element or concept are you adding to your products? What new feature are you adding to your services? How are you helping to solve your clients' problems? Or how are you preventing clients' problems from happening in the first place? Is it by using or designing the right products and services and leveraging the right technology?

These are the factors that need to be considered. Hence, it is of paramount importance to hire and attract the right set of people to work for you. Not everyone has the same capabilities and abilities. Individual skills differ. One must be able to figure out who is good at what in the very beginning to eradicate poor performance in the latter days. When all individual skill sets are categorized, then a team leader can streamline on building the right team with the right people. Having the wrong people in the right role is like having a square peg in a round hole. To drive high performance, you must have the right people in the right role.

Very often, people are given roles that are not aligned to their aspirations or skill sets. And that creates a lot of dissatisfaction, and it does not let people perform to their potential. Of course, it is equally important to ensure that your employees stay with you. You can retain their drive and energy to surpass their achieved goals and ensure that they remain self-motivated to exceed their existing plans. When all the teammates work collectively toward their set objectives and the team's goals with high motivation, it is easier to achieve their goals. Constant communication is needed to make sure that they are on track and are not facing any troubles. Continuous development and upgrading of your skills, and continuously changing the benchmark of your standards, be it benchmarking for best practices in the industry or best practices in the organization, or creating your own new best practices, which could be from outside the industry, are all key factors you need to keep cultivating. A key attribute in a high-performing team, as I have stressed frequently, is not being satisfied with the status quo.

Cultivate seeing failures as learning lessons. I treat it as an opportunity to become better in the future. Failure should be considered as a stepping stone to success, especially when it comes to organizations. Create a culture where people are able to speak their minds; create a culture where people are able to accept their failures.

This should involve a sense of security, but not complacency. People learn from their failures, so let them learn and let them not make the same mistake twice. But encourage them to be honest enough and own up when they make mistakes.

The attempt and the willingness to try something will have a lot of positive impact on the skillset even if people do not succeed. It is no secret that many successful entrepreneurs had to taste failures first before turning out to be what they are today. In fact, they embrace their failures as proudly as they do their successes. Take the example of Steve Jobs, who was an impressive entrepreneur because of his boundless innovations and his unbelievable comeback from an almost irrecoverable failure. Jobs found success in his twenties when Apple became a massive empire, but when he was 30 years old, Apple's board of directors decided to fire him. Without letting the pain overtake him, Jobs founded a new company NeXT, which was eventually acquired by Apple. Once back at Apple, he showed the world what he was capable of doing.

Resilience is a fundamental quality of cultural traits. All businesses go through highs and lows. What matters is how focused you are when you go through your lows. How complacent are you in your good times? Do you often find yourself getting too comfortable in your zone? These are the questions one needs to contemplate on. Of course, that does not mean you should not savor your wins. There is nothing quite like success.

Every small win and every small challenge which one overcomes drives teams to perform in a bigger and better way. Every small victory leads us closer to the winning post. Each victory should be celebrated. Treat failures as a learning opportunity rather than allowing them to get the better of you.

I would say in terms of cultural traits, normalize people collaborating, supporting, and respecting each other as individuals and learning from each other, and getting each other to overcome their gaps.

This is why motivating everyone in the team is indeed a big step. If they do not have the clarity that their achievements will also be counted, then there is a high chance that they are working just to fill the gap and not with their whole heart. The team should be aware that failing to achieve even a single person's target will impact the team's growth. Rather than getting into a culture of finger-pointing and blaming each other when things go wrong, employees should be encouraged to inspire each other. The culture of organizational politics, pulling each other down, and the absence of support should be avoided. Often, indulging in blame games and drawing the other person down are critical reasons for not driving high performance.

When you take responsibility for your mistakes and own up to them, your employees will follow as well. An employee satisfaction score will help you understand the limitations and derailers that impact the building of your high-performance team. We can always go back and forth and address them by making changes in policies and processes, as well as in leadership styles.

It is important to exhibit these traits on a regular and continuous basis, and every team member should demonstrate that they are living, eating, and breathing this culture. It is great if one is able to do this consistently, and there is no reason why you cannot surpass your expected goals.

Ensuring productivity, anticipating issues in advance, and early risk-taking, taking calculated risks, and having a plan B in place— this is what a high-performing individual's checklist looks like. Now, what would come in the way of driving high performance is complacency or getting into a comfort zone. Try to ensure not only continuous learning and development but also focus on rewards and recognition, that is, rewarding high performance and celebrating successes. We must not forget to look at performance goals and rewards. Organizations have introduced many schemes such as innovation schemes and employee recognition schemes.

At the beginning of the month or the beginning of the quarter, an employee appreciation scheme is put in place.
Let us consider the following case study.

CASE STUDY:

I would like to talk about an organization, particularly a mid-sized organization, which had a legacy of about 15 years. It was run by a third-generation entrepreneur and was into manufacturing and had a list of global clients. The key strength of this organization was its strong legacy.

However, the products offered used outdated technology, which meant the cost of production was high and not in keeping with the current rates. It also had an aging workforce, with employees working beyond the age of retirement, which meant that newer ideas were not being implemented. In the workforce, a sense of complacency had taken over the people. Although the customers were being retained, with about 80% client retention, there was no growth.

Eventually, the organization was forced to undertake a costly restructuring exercise due to business circumstances, increased competition, and clients looking for alternate vendor requirements. The organization was now looking into driving growth by creating a culture of high performance. They wanted to create the right kind of enablers to enhance profitability and growth. An important element to achieve this was having a clear strategy. The organization engaged us as a consultant, and we were able to provide input into the business strategy. We started with the model of strategy, structure, and culture and looked to integrate the three to drive business growth. So, the strategy laid out a clear five-year roadmap for the organization. We checked that the roadmap was on the right track by doing a PESTLE analysis.

PESTLE here stands for political, economic, social, technological, legal, and environmental factors. This analysis allows one to visualize the impact of these factors on their industry. PESTLE analysis helps in a major way to anticipate reactionary elements and to prepare accordingly. SWOT analysis is another tool that is very commonly used not only by businesses but by individuals as well. SWOT stands for Strength, Weaknesses, Opportunities, and Threats. This analysis gives one a wonderful insight into themselves. Self-awareness is the key to exceeding performance. While SWOT analysis presents an opportunity to look both inward and outward, PESTLE analysis is a chance to explore all your external options. So that is what we did. Post that, we also improvised on the seven frameworks to drive business strategy.

Once we had the strategy in place, we looked at creating the right organizational design. This meant clearly reducing the spans, optimizing the layers, defining key roles and accountabilities, and right-sizing the numbers. This helped the organization to such a great extent. We started the process with a zero-based approach, which was linked to the strategy of today, current realities, and the desired outcome in five years. One of the key findings here was that the organization was overstaffed at too many layers, which included, one on one recordings and better-defined roles and responsibilities.

We started by correcting the structure of the organization and defining spans, years, and components. We also defined what the delegation of authority levels was. Delegation of authority is an important factor because authority is defined as rights inherent in a managerial position to give orders and expect the orders to be obeyed. Delegation of authority is the process by which managers allocate the authority down to the people who report to them. It involves the handling of responsibility and power. When authority is delegated suitably, it leads to empowerment. We found that the managers were not creating the right kind of enablers. They were not giving feedback on time, giving coaching, or giving development opportunities. "What managers believe about themselves subtly influences what they believe about their subordinates, what they expect of them, and how they treat them." The above quote clearly throws light on the importance of a manager's or a coach's mindset when it comes to the development of a high-performance team.

Surprisingly, when we looked into fitting the right people in the room, we found that about 80% of the workforce was not suited to play in the business going ahead. That did not mean that we had to replace 80% of the workforce immediately. But it was required to be done in phases. We placed the people into three categories:

- People who fitted into the succession planning grid
- People with low performance and low potential
- People with low performance and moderate potential.

We gave up on those with low performance and low potential, which was about 10% of the workforce. But to balance it out, we invested in training and developing the inconsistent performers and the average performers. It is the responsibility of the coach to mold his coachees and bring out the best in them.

A mentor is a person who can bring his mentee to the proper shape, help him reorder his priorities, and help him achieve his targets. In a way, the coach should closely work with his team to keep them motivated and engaged and more focused on their work. Clients should be made comfortable with the way their coach has mutual respect for everyone and should tackle issues of any sort of disharmony in a smooth manner. The main focus here was setting clear goals for them based on their performance and the management objectives. Their performance was categorized into four different levels:

(i)   managing business performance, process, and compliance
(ii) driving productivity
(iii) efficiency
(iv) building organization capability and talent. These were the four broad areas where the goals were set, and they were all aligned to the CEO's goals. Interdependence of goals between various functions was established, and weightages were assigned.

This process gave the employees a sense of clarity in terms of what they needed to do. This was reviewed on a monthly basis, and we saw growth at a CAGR of 25% happening year after year for the business. The transformation that happened to this organization was not magic. It did not happen overnight. It was the step-by-step execution of a detailed plan customized to their strengths and weaknesses. In creating a high-performance culture, I think a holistic approach, right from setting performance goals and establishing clarity, is necessary.

Doing a series of interventions that promotes a sense of ownership and accountability in driving the culture of trust and collaboration between various departments is a major indicator of success.

TAKEAWAYS:

- Considering the case study we have discussed, we can see it is people who drove performance. It is people who drive innovation.
- Earlier, there was no innovation coming in, and people felt they were rewarded only for showing up at work. Initially, there was a lot of resistance in implementing the scheme. But gradually, when people started seeing success, they started turning things around.
- The turnaround that happened came through because we had a clear strategy in place. We were able to achieve it because of the right organizational structure and the right people in the right roles.
- It is essential to drive a culture of ownership and accountability.
- Having the right process of performance management integrates goal setting, which in turn integrates review or performance. This can be supported by coaching and development.

- It is important to define behavioral changes, and communicating this to everybody in a way that they understand clearly would certainly up the game. This provides a way to monitor the progress in shifting the culture. The behavior that individuals possess should be closely related to their work front.
- Discovering the exact mindset: It is very crucial to analyze the employee's perspective, where he sees himself in the forthcoming years, and what kind of growth he wants to see in himself. Only after this is clear can an organization's head plan accordingly. Not just finding it out but also reframing it is very necessary.
- Making people understand the importance of getting influenced. Being influenced by a colleague or somebody associated with the field is not a bad thing at all. Employees should learn how to incorporate certain behaviors from people around them if they feel that it could up their game at work. One should not be embarrassed to appreciate a good idea.
- Executing a program where each level works in harmony forms a coherent experience for employees, and there it minimizes confusion and accelerates the transition to a new culture, especially a high-performing culture. Providing incentives, recognition, and appreciation of their work.
- Producing opportunities for individuals to overcome personal barriers. For organizations to change, people must change. But that is not easy since everyone possesses a different level of willingness and ability to change. An additional level of approach must be followed with each individual to make sure one gets the motivation to come out of their barriers and work hard for the organization.
- Lead the journey in employee-centric ways: Instead of looking at everything from a managerial or top-down approach, it is imperative to see through the eyes of employees.

CONCLUSION

They say every ending is a new beginning. We may have reached the end of this book, but this is only the beginning to what I hope is a wonderful start to forming your very own success story of delivering high performance. **Let us walk through some important areas of what we have discussed.**

WHAT CONSTITUTES A HIGH-PERFORMING TEAM?

- Firstly, a high-performing team has a very high sense of purpose and a sense of commitment to achieve aligned goals.
- A long-term vision also inspires high-performing teams. They do not work only for achieving the key result areas. They do not look at narrow job descriptions that have very limited key result areas. They go beyond that. They have a deeper sense of purpose, a deeper understanding of alignment to contribute to a bigger cause.
- High-performing teams are benchmarks. They urge the best people to want to be a part of the team. It is about attracting the right people and exciting people who would simply like to stay and dedicate themselves for a long time.
- The fourth part here is that a high-performing team continuously keeps raising the bar of performance.

- They make every year a better year. They not only surpass the benchmarks, but they actively create new benchmarks for their level of performance. That is what high performance is all about, to not only achieve standards but surpass and create new benchmarks. Consider the 100 meters sprint: previously, 20 seconds was a great record, now it has come down to 10 seconds. It sounds almost impossible, but that is the reality. And that is the exact effect a high-performing team has on people. Every year you see that performance keeps increasing unbelievably, and records keep breaking.
- A high-performing team is based on culture—a culture based on trust where team members stand by each other and collaborate. They are there to help each other rather than find faults and enter into a blame game.
- High-performing teams continue. They go on. They are all about development. They continuously and consciously invest in it, making an effort to upgrade their technical, behavioral, managerial, or leadership skills.
- High-performing culture is also about celebrating success. High-performing teams find ways of celebrating success. Every achievement is a true reflection of good quality teamwork. Credit is shared with the entire team. It is about each member playing their role and acknowledging the position which each member has played. That is what we call celebrating success. It is not about the parties. Parties are something that can be done any which way. But here, what matters is the thought and action of recognizing the contribution of every member in a success. No matter how big or small, it is for the organization.
- The other important area of your performance culture is encouraging a culture of taking calculated risks and not admonishing failures or mistakes. It is about learning from those mistakes.
- And ensuring that the same error does not get repeated.

WHY TEAMS FAIL TO BECOME HIGH-PERFORMING TEAMS:

- Failure starts with the lack of accountability and ownership.

Passing blame to the next person should not be allowed, and team members should be encouraged to say, "Yes, it happened. We need to own this issue together and work toward solving it."

- Lack of aligned goals and a sense of purpose also leads to disintegration.
- Lack of specific standards of performance or standards of performance being very vague leads to confusion and misunderstanding of a goal.
- Lack of training and development is another mistake. If you keep doing the same job in the same way, you will not raise your bar of performance.
  How do you continuously keep sharpening your skills?
- Another part of this is the fear of failure and being admonished for taking calculated risks.
- Also, organizational politics can be extremely dangerous to high-performing teams. They can be highly detrimental in terms of encouraging a culture of performance and meritocracy.
- Not having the right leadership skills that encourage diversity and inclusion by having different team members with different experiences, backgrounds, and skills also leads to failure.
- It is important to have a team working toward a common sense of purpose, driving a culture of inclusion, and ensuring that team members can contribute and are given the right roles.
- Conflict can contribute constructively. Differences of opinion are bound to arise in the workplace, but it is important to ensure that either there is a convergence in ideas or an amicable 'agree to disagree' policy.
- Lack of shared vision and rewards can also lead to the disintegration of teams.

These are a few areas that the team needs to watch out for.

KEY INGREDIENTS TO FORM A HIGH-PERFORMING TEAM:

- It begins by hiring right. It is about ensuring that you can attract the right people to your team.

That comes by guaranteeing a clear sense of purpose, effective communication, and transparency.

- It also comes from your internal team members being strong advocates of your brand. Today, there is a lot of social media activity. And although I do not subscribe to certain activities on social media platforms, people talk about either positive or negative feedback. I do not personally subscribe to that because social media is not the best way of handling that. But great teams, through word of mouth, turn out to be extremely strong advocates. For attracting the right kind of people and great team members, the high performers revealing their experience may come off as an honest, unofficial advertisement of your brand, which will attract the right kind of talent. High-performing members in your team are mostly very good advocates, and they can truly be your active spokespeople.
- Post-hiring, having a sense of purpose, setting clear goals, that is, specific, measurable, attainable, and result-oriented goals, and effective communication with authenticity and transparency are crucial. They are the key components of what makes the team, and there is no substitute for that. With clarity and a sense of purpose, you will be able to build a high-performing team quite easily.
- A sense of purpose is an exceptional quality in leaders. Often, I have seen leaders who communicate budgets and numbers. People are not attracted to budgets or numbers; they are drawn to a purpose beyond the budgets and numbers, and it is your responsibility to give them that.
- Continuous development and training, again, are the core of high-performing teams. One needs to keep sharpening the sword continuously. Review and recalibrate training needs and development consistently. Creating and ensuring a high-performance culture of trust, collaboration, mutual respect, diversity, and inclusion is in place.
- By diversity, we talk about creating a culture of meritocracy where people of different backgrounds, strengths, and experiences want to work with you and are excited to stay with you and perform.

- It is also equally important to include them in terms of taking key decisions, be it providing the right kind of inputs, bouncing ideas off, or setting mutually aligned goals. Diversity and inclusivity cannot exist without each other.

WHAT KEEPS A HIGH-PERFORMING TEAM TOGETHER?

- The main key here is consistency. You have to set clear standards about what constitutes good performance, what constitutes outstanding performance, and what constitutes underperformance, and what are the consequences associated with each of them. This ensures that there is clarity and inspires people to achieve high performance.
- At the same time, it also ensures everyone supports each other. Teams need an understanding that they are aligned not only to individual targets but also to team targets. Individuals should be able to align to their personal goals as well as to the goals of the other members of the team.
This will foster an environment of trust and collaboration, driving the right kind of behavior.
- Achieving the same targets will not inspire growth and high performance. It will encourage people to get stuck in a comfort zone. So, keeping a slight element of stretch but with a word of caution can aid in high performance.
- A thumb rule that I follow is that the human mind can achieve more than 20%-25% (it is an indicative number and can be a higher or lower percentage) of what we are currently performing. If we put our mind to it, we will find ways to achieve it.
- Promoting the right leadership culture, as I mentioned, involves diversity and inclusion, setting clear goals, defining a sense of purpose, and ensuring that everyone knows that rewards and consequences are aligned to high-performance. And the use of a combination of financial and non-financial motivators should sustain a high-performing team.

All of these points should help you understand, build, grow, and sustain a high-performing team. Finally, I would like to quote Harvey MacKay here:

"People begin to become successful the minute they decide to be."

Victories are not born out of thin air. It takes patience and consistent effort. It takes rigorous training, resilience, strength, and action. High performance starts with the mind and ends with the heart.

A high-performing team is simply a set of people who wake up and choose to chase that dream, that goal—a bunch of people who wake up every day and decide to be successful.

The question is, are you one of them?

REFERENCES

I

https://hbr.org/2017/03/teams-solve-problems-faster-when-theyre-more-cognitively-diverse

https://www.cnbc.com/2021/03/04/zoom-doordash-peloton-led-fastest-growing-tech-companies-in-2020.html

II

https://hbr.org/2019/05/your-approach-to-hiring-is-all-wrong

III

https://hbr.org/2019/05/your-approach-to-hiring-is-all-wrong

IV

https://www.bizjournals.com/bizjournals/how-to/growth-strategies/2014/12/what-a-nasa-janitor-can-teach-us.html

VII

https://www.gallup.com/workplace/236366/right-culture-not-employee-satisfaction.aspx

https://www.workstyle.io/top-performing-team-case-studies

Royal Society – Wikipedia (https://en.wikipedia.org/wiki/Royal_Society)

XII

Leadership 101 For Entrepreneurs, From Chhatrapati Shivaji Maharaj (inc42.com) (https://inc42.com/resources/leadership-101-for-entrepreneurs-from-chhatrapati-shivaji-maharaj/)

Shivaji – Wikipedia
(https://en.wikipedia.org/wiki/Shivaji#Early_life)

The Successors of Shivaji: Detailed Overview (jagranjosh.com)
(https://www.jagranjosh.com/general-knowledge/the-successors-of-shivaji-1442578007-1)

10 Most Famous Indian Kings and Emperors - Discover Walks Blog
(https://www.discoverwalks.com/blog/india/10-most-famous-indian-kings-and-emperors/)

ABOUT THE AUTHOR

Ajay Bakshi is a senior HR, and business transformation thought leader, executive coach, and organization development coach to CEOs, CXOs, emerging leaders of MNC, public sector undertakings, family-run business, and government sectors. He enables building and transforming organizations and careers by integrating organization strategy, structure, culture, and leadership by creating high performing teams.

He counts MIT Manipal and Pune University as his alma mater. With over 30 years of experience, Ajay is a PCC (Professional Certified Coach) executive and business coach from ICF, USA, with over 5,000 coaching hours under his belt.

Ajay has been widely recognized for his contributions in the HR sector. He has won several awards, including *Performance Coach by Economic Times in July 2021*, *HR Consultant and Executive Coach by Economic Times in December 2021*, *Best Global HR Strategy*, *Company of The Year*, *MSME Best Consulting Company*, and many other awards. He has also been featured in *Economic Times*, *Business Today*, *Forbes India*, *and Fortune India* in 2021 for the work done in transforming businesses and people.

Please scan the QR code to know more about Ajay Bakshi.

www.ingramcontent.com/pod-product-compliance
Lightning Source LLC
LaVergne TN
LVHW011416080426
835512LV00005B/87